"I Am Not Your Black, America!"

MeShorn T. Floyd-Daniels

Uncle MeShorn

www.UncleMeShorn.com

Copyright © 2023 by Trient Press

All rights reserved. No part of this publication may be reproduced, distributed, or transmitted in any form or by any means, including photocopying, recording, or other electronic or mechanical methods, without the prior written permission of the publisher, except in the case of brief quotations embodied in critical reviews and certain other noncommercial uses permitted by copyright law. For permission requests, write to the publisher, addressed "Attention: Permissions Coordinator," at the address below.

Criminal copyright infringement, including infringement without monetary gain, is investigated by the FBI and is punishable by up to five years in federal prison and a fine of $250,000.

Except for the original story material written by the author, all songs, song titles, and lyrics mentioned in the novel I Am Not Your Black, America! are the exclusive property of the respective artists, songwriters, and copyright holder.

Trient Press
3375 S Rainbow Blvd
#81710, SMB 13135
Las Vegas, NV 89180

Ordering Information:
Quantity sales. Special discounts are available on quantity purchases by corporations, associations, and others. For details, contact the publisher at the address above.
Orders by U.S. trade bookstores and wholesalers. Please contact Trient Press: Tel: (775) 996-3844; or visit www.trientpress.com.

Printed in the United States of America

Publisher's Cataloging-in-Publication data
Floyd-Daniels, MeShorn T.
A title of a book : I Am Not Your Black, America!
ISBN

Hard Cover	979-8-88990-126-6
Paper Back	979-8-88990-127-3
Ebook	979-8-88990-128-0
Large Print Paperback	979-8-88990-153-2

"I have a dream: That one day on the red hills of Georgia, the sons of former slaves and the sons of former slave owners will be able to sit together at the table of brotherhood."

Martin Luther King, Jr.

Acknowledgments

I begin with all humbleness, deeply grateful to many people that I'd like to acknowledge. Before all else, I would like to be clear on this point: I intend to be as honest and transparent as possible regarding this project, as it would be totally irresponsible, reckless, and fraudulent of me not to express thanks and appreciation where due.

Thus, firstly, I want to acknowledge my writersand the entire Urban Publishing team connected to this project. They absolutely and astutely understood and embraced the entire truth of Uncle Me'Shorn; not once did they raise any objection to my ideas, nor did they attempt to manipulate or push me away from being my authentic self. Instead of trying to change my truth, they embodied it – they *listened* and drew inspiration from the same wellspring of divine principles my own thoughts came from. They also countered any limitations present in my own prose, as it presented unique challenges due to theuse of Ebonics; sometimes, they would require phone conferences to decode my written literature since it was certainly written in an unorthodox style, one perhaps even unintelligible to many others. Yet, they always tried to maintain my voice and perspectives in the text, especially with regard to my personal history and plights.

I believe they actually felt my heart as I attempted to reach a new level of strength to overcome the hurdles in our path. Conversing with the writers, my confidence in the project grew; even though there was certainly a generational and linguistic gap between us, we overcame these barriers to understanding. Had we simply accepted these hurdles as fact, this project would perhaps never have come about.

In this book, I have unapologetically represented a clear identity of myself as a proud descendant of African American slaves. Yet, my narrative is not racial; it is the narrative of humanism and humanity itself, written from the perspective of a man who is a member of the Baby Boomer generation, born between in mid-1960 to 1964. Conversing with my writers, I was undoubtedly their Elder; nonetheless, we relatively understood and shared a certain sameness of identity and character, having been born in America in a similar epoch, one that has stretched from 1960 to the present moment of the 21st century

I am convinced that there was perhaps no way to have received some keen insights had it not been for the keen interest shown by the writers, who did their best to listen, understand, encourage, and support the thoughts I wanted to put to paper. Ultimately, I would say the team as a whole was a big part of bringing this project to completion.

***

I would also like to give homage and acknowledgment to my ancestors, to whom I owe my present life. Ye (Kanye West) said slavery in America was a choice; in response, the American Black persecuted him as a sellout, labeled him as crazy, and claimed that he needed help. But if

today's generation of the American Black has never

seen the movie Amistad, they are basically ignorant of the Africans who chose not to be Slaves. It was these folk who were freed by legendary former president of the United States of America, John Adams – he defended them and allowed them to return home to Africa. They were cleared of all charges despite killing almost everyone on that ship that had captured and enslaved them.

They were enslaved, but they chose not to be slaves.

Slavery is a choice. Many made the decision to commit suicide and die; others decided to live, to create a social lineage. Consequently, their lives mattered to the blood generation that came after them. I am descended from this lineage.

I am honored to be a seedling from my Grandfather, a King on my Mother's side, and my Grandmother, who was a Queen on my Father's side. To my Mother, Hattie Laura Conley Floyd Daniels, I am thankful for these four specific things: Life. Name. Shelter from
black Churches. A place in the Army

**

I would also like to acknowledge the Queen to my status as King: my Wife, Jacqueline E Daniels. She is the Queen who showed her importance to me spectacularly through her actions after our marriage. She took the great revelation given unto her about the man she had married and gave me a perspective regarding how naïve and ignorant I was about white and black Christianity. There were astonishing challenges to overcome in the year 2006 during the Louisville Peace Festival, but she stood by me resolutely. She served a key role in my life as a most vulnerable figure who helped me realize the fullest potential of my Self, helping me become Who I Am. I am sincerely blessed and fortunate to have selected this angel of a woman placed by God at the Crossroads of my self-discovery.

To her, I can only say a phrase from a song by George Huff:

I Can Count On You.

***

I am also appreciative of the opportunities to Learn, Unlearn, and Relearn provided by my Family members, who endured me, even if they didn't have any clue regarding the role they played in the completion of this project.

The blood Family members I would first thank are Charles E. Daniels, Melissa Floyd, and their Children – my nieces and nephews. Thank you, all.

But there is more to family. After a startling discovery through Ancestry.com, I was able to reconnect with my 102-year-old Grandma in Miami, Florida: Lilly Bell Floyd. I was separated fifty-five years ago from her when I was just a five- year-old. Also reconnecting with me are my little brother, Trevor Floyd, and his wife – this concluding my Family on the side of my Father, Clyde Me'Shorn Floyd. But there are multiple other blood Family members to mention, such as my cousins Hope, Contrell, Keisha, and many more, too numerous to mention.

***

But then, there are the many adopted Family members. Though they and I share no bond of blood, I could not have achieved as much as I have without their support.

First among my adopted Family is the US Army – where I became myself, and developed my natural roots and Manhood. The Army is what led to me becoming a surgical technologist. The pathways in my life were perhaps decided by the drilled sergeants of Fort Jackson and the men in South Carolina – SFC Fry and 1st Sgt. Hunter.

Back at the 98th General Hospital, West Germany, thanks to my roommate Robert Edwards, my section manager SFC Zeb Wilmington and Sergeant Major Jefferson, who set on my promotion board to becoming a Sergeant First Class / SFC.

And I've not forgotten Terry Miner, WHAS Radio 840 AM. He is my Brother, a man who gave me airwave times in Louisville, Kentucky, over twenty or more times… Call it an epiphany, but if I had to guess and place money on it, Terry had to

very carefully choose how to navigate the situation whenever my name came up!

Terry is a classy individual – he'd never admit it, but he openly, unapologetically, and publicly introduced me to this city as if we were Brothers from different Mothers.

Finally, thanks to High School homeboys and classmates Alvin Breedlove, and K C Anderson.

They were clueless of the childhood horrors I lived with, but nonetheless allowed me to follow in their footsteps.

***

I would also like to acknowledge the many members of the nursing staff, the physicians, and all those working in the Surgical Service University of Louisville Hospital that I owe so much to.

Here are just a few professional colleagues who have left a lasting impression on me: firstly, Dr.

James, chief surgery, Ft Hood Texas. The University of Louisville medical community served me the greatest initially; Dr. Greg Nazar, Dr.

Rafeal Cruz, Dr. Timir Banerjee, Dr. John Sansbury, Dr Smith Chairman of Surgical Services, Dr. Franklin chief of trauma, Dr. Miller, Dr. David Seligson, Dr Hartley, Dr. Cho, Dr Bozeman, Dr Harbrecht, Dr Roberts the Chairman orthopedic services at University of Louisville Orthopedic, and countless more…The University of Louisville Hospital Surgery Nursing Staff but, more specifically Debbie Judd, Kathy Robinson, Chase, Josie, Corey, Kathy, Angie, Nolan, Josh, Jamie, Bro. Sam, Jenny, Mike one & two, Marty Pam, Raven and Patty, Shayla, John, Jeremy, Megan, The Irish orthopedic nurse Sioban Victory, Faithia Cain, Julie Lamount, Sherry, Celeste, Melissa Johnson, Donna, Donnie, Abraham Donald, The orthopedic reps: Logan, Connor , and memory of Phil,The Jenny &, Allen, My friends Lee Wilson, Reyonna Gill from Norton's, Kim B (OR girlfriend), laVerne (My cougar), Ian, Debbie Whitening, Elaine Strong and Sue Ann Carrillo (My work Wife Queen)

The above were all, perhaps, the most significant peoples who help in my development in Louisville, Ky.

***

I would also like to reach out with the deepest gratitude to all the organizations, authors, movements, and individuals listed here:

Primerica

Mike and Jenny, Wallace and Gillia, Rick and Carol, and Patrica and Nita

MAN UP USA

Adolph Thompson, Ray Barker, Martin Smith, Steve Petrey, Rick Holland, Jeremiah Morton, and Mike Craven.

HISTORY UNTOLD 400

HistoryUntold400.org

Leonard Walker, Peter Hayes, and Shahram Sedehi mediajoy.org – who has now become my Sergeant major in finishing the publishing of this book.

TRUTHE BE TOLD

TrutheBeTold.com

Marcus Ray Joe Trapper, Ray Ali God's Lives Matter GodsLivesMatter.com

Frank Porter, Charles E. Daniels, Gidget Muhammad (Queen), and Mertus Strong, – and if it wasn't for my Daughter Andrea Denise Daniels, is the inspiration for God's Lives Matter GLM.

I didn't know the plan's but I'm glad God knew.

Vanessa Simagan is my special big Sister and a feminine spiritual friend. She was much needed by me and seemed to stand with me in all my endeavors, even when she didn't agree with or share my politics. Yet I salute Vanessa's willingness to give me her ear and her patience to travel with me on the journey of writing this book!

To Pastor Bob Rogers (Evangel World Church):

"Sir, you are truly a man of God. You never once put any restrictions on our relationship. As part of the 2006 Louisville Peace Festival, you kept your word to support me when I invited my guest, George Huff from American Idol, to be interviewed by WJIE Radio and your congregation showed up on the Waterfront to make the event happen."

To Rev. Sun Myung Moon (Heavenly Parents Holy Community):

"Immediately after my 2006 Peace Festival and after reading Dr Norris Shelton's America's Little Black Book, I met you in Washington, DC. Even though married for ten years, I still had so much to learn about what is the purpose of marriage and life. Then, you blessed my marriage as you ministered to us, that God's original intention for this world has been to raise healthy and happy families. The memory of our encounter never fades! Thank you!

America's Little Black Book - ALBB

This book and its author provided language and literature that was foundational to my own endeavors; its guidance helped me understand my own prior struggles and battles with mischaracterized emotions and the depression that domesticated black folks

My thanks to Dr. Norris Shelton, James Elliott, and Carl Hamilton.

American Slavery

Dr. Gerald Higginbotham was invited to come from St Louis, MO, into my life. When I was about to walk away, he anchored me to the understanding that there was, indeed, a purpose as to why ALBB was written.

***

At the end of this acknowledgment, it is important to me that I show the depth of my gratitude. It is hard to imagine the level of discipline, strength, and compassion needed to be my core through thick and thin. There were times when I found myself in some rough emotional spots – there were dark and painful times, times when I was screwed over, abused, and cheated by the hands of others....

It was a great, comforting relief – and indeed, comfort and relief – to hear the all-encompassing message of God's love that visited me in my car.

When I spoke in tongues, the utterance gave me solace in a moment of loneliness and desolation; it was then that I gained my wit, acquiring all the acronyms you'll find throughout my book.

One acronym you won't find anywhere else but here is L.OV.E; it is the very first emotion I felt when I received Him. L.OV.E stands for Love Overcomes Everything – and that is true for both divine love and that which I received from all those around me.

I found love, and thus, I overcame.

***

And last, but certainly never least: my thanks to my foster-father Charles E. Daniels, who is a King who rose above indecision. I specifically acknowledge him here for specific purposes familiar only to all those who have traveled in astute and spiritual deep waters.

Thank you for being my Dad, and an exemplary

American Man, Husband, and Father who found his way and took responsibility.

Lastly, thanks to Dr Shawn Gardner (2NOT1.org) for taking my photo for the cover of this book.

***

This book is just my individual W.O.R.K.
Acronym Wisdom, Opportunity, Respect (responsibility) and Knowledge

My heartfelt thanks to you all.

Contents

Preface	
Part I	
Beginnings	
Not Your Black	
Roots	
Who I Am	
Early Years	
Skeletons	
Louisville	
Part II	
Paradigms	
Color Construct	
Uncle Tom	
Your 'Great' America	
Control	
T.O.O.L.S. and W.O.R.K	
Part III	
Beliefs	

	Epiphany	
	B.I.B.L.E	
	American Faith	
	God's Lives Matter	
	Part IV	
	Families	
	The Future Family	
	King and Queen	
	Moving Forward	
	Part V	
	Endings	
	Epilogue	
	Appendix	
	Table Of Content	

Preface

---
*"I am **not** your negro."*

James Baldwin

In a 1968 interview on The Dick Cavett Show, Cavett notes that Baldwin is often asked a stubborn question: "Why aren't the Negroes optimistic?"

He says that many people believe the situation to be improving considerably, with 'black' people now holding positions of influence across society: as mayors, professional athletes, politicians and TV actors. Cavett asks Baldwin, "Is it at once getting much better and still hopeless?"

In response, Baldwin says, "I don't think there's much hope for it, as long as people are using this peculiar language. It's not a question of what happens to the Negro here, [though] that is a very vivid question for me." Baldwin continues to assert that the fate of the United States is directly linked to how effectively it addresses the plight of Black Americans.

***

Baldwin's argument is what I, Me'Shorn T. Floyd Daniels, seek to represent in context of the 21st century, which brings with it its own challenges.

It's my belief that my book is a reflection of the conclusion reached by James Baldwin – however, this book also draws from all the epiphanies that were my immediate horrors once I matured and wandered away from my innocence.

Similarly to James Baldwin, I, too, saw many problems and horrific issues that remained unresolved. This state of affairs, I realized, was no different than what occurred in the Beginning – it echoed the events that took place in the Garden with the first man and woman, as recounted in Genesis. They, too, lost their innocence and became aware; they gained the knowledge of their nakedness. They realized a state of shame.

The humanity that was once cared for as an innocent sparrow fell from its lofty perch and began to move towards an immediate and inexorable course leading unto Death. Now, everything that would happen to Humans moving forward would come solely on the basis of our "Wisdom, Opportunity, Responsibility (Respect) and Knowledge – and this is how I came to the acronym, W.O.R.K.

This, I found, was the only way to overcome the punishment humanity was sentenced to for life on earth.

Our fate, identification, and answers were to come through the hearts and blood of each individual. We all have the ability to overcome the challenge put forth to us on this earth – we must all lead by example, astutely applying our free will as Men, Husbands, Fathers, or as

Women, Wives and Mothers on this grand board game of earth.

We all carry an element of agency when navigating the global matrix we were born into.

Even in the beginning, through a child's understanding, I realized that the world around me and the things I experienced in my path were extremely dysfunctional, unnatural, and oddly distorted. And thus, Uncle Me'Shorn navigated an interesting, complex matrix, what I eventually learned to call a dominant majority environment.

This is what I discovered in my medical profession, specifically in the Operating Room as a surgical technologist trained in the US Army: the hospital and medical profession industry is like any other business in America. It is a capitalist system primarily focused on generating profits.

It's now been more than forty years, and to my surprise, I discovered that I had been indoctrinated, domesticated, and pushed into docility – I had been quarantined and sheltered. I had not learned the tactics and strategy required for the chess-game of the color construct. However, I subverted the rules of this game by introducing the game of Bid Whist, a game I taught myself in West Germany. I learned to call my trumps and play my hands, and I was able to learn to unlearn to relearn. I began to clearly see the situation of all those born before 1960; being born speaking after the Civil Rights movement and after the explosive success of MLK's I Have A Dream speech, I grew to become a surgical technologist. Alone in the midst of a dominant majority environment, I became a King in the Operating Room – a King among Kings and Queens.

But if you want to identify yourself as a King or Queen, you must astutely grasp the fact that the chessboard of Europeans democracy is specifically created for the King and Queen. As the original seedling in a St. Louis Court once said,

"The white man and government they created for white Americans have no reason to respect or honor anything or anyone who identifies as blacks

– those who they name and classify as slaves."

So, as a Man who belongs to a descendant-demographic systematically created for white Kings and Queens, my first obligation is to become my own King and identify my Queen.

And that is why:

I am not your black, America.

Part I
Beginnings

Not Your Black.

> *"A man dies when he refuses to stand up for that which is **right**. A man dies when he refuses to stand up for **justice**. A man dies when he refuses to take a stand for that which is **true**."*

Martin Luther King, Jr.

I begin by saying again:

I am not your black, America.

What is Your Black? Let me answer you; it sits in the nooks and crannies of your societies. It languishes in the hood, in the ghettoes upholding your endless skyscrapers. Your Black provides you with an endless supply of labor without a penny's cost; Your Black sits in the prisons, feeding a military-industrial complex that never stops. Your Black is an idea, amorphous and easy to apply or withdraw; what is 'Black' today is universal tomorrow.

Your Black is without meaning. It is shaped by carrots and sticks, false hopes, and prison walls.

It is a representation, and I am not – my name is Me'Shorn Tyrone Floyd Daniels, and I refuse to fit into your construct. I am not merely a color, and I am not a race-identity for you to construct; I am a man. You cannot make me anything other than who I am.

You clamor to represent me and the rest of us in your media, in the stories devised by you and for you, yet, the flaw is in the name. Representation; it is only a surface-image, nothing but an illusion you perpetuate at your pleasure. I am not your lie; I am the truth underneath.

I am not your representation of me. I am the self you have repressed like a bad memory.

But America, I have still loved you. Despite it all, I have loved you, believed in you, and served for you. I gave you twenty-one years of my life in service. I am not your enemy, for I am among your truest friends. Ask yourself: who is a better friend? Someone who supports you without question, even when you are in grievous error? Or someone who stops you in the middle of wrongdoing and tries to guide you towards a better path?

I am of the second sort. Some flatterer, I am not. A sycophant, I am not.

If I seem unduly harsh in my appraisal of you, America, it is because I love you. If I seem unfair in judging you, it is because you have rarely been fair with me, either. And if I seem to be angry, remember that I speak from passion, not hate – for I disavow hate, in all its forms. Hate is what has brought us so low; only love can make us rise again.

I do not hate the white for being white. I do not hate the rich for being rich. I am not an everyday reactionary here to spew and sow bad blood – God knows there's enough of that already. I am only here to give you my two cents and a word of advice, but if I have to shout to make myself heard, you can bet I will. I am not Your Black – my ideology does not follow the narratives you have constructed. You have presented your people with a pop-quiz version of dissent: "Please pick this narrative if you are black". I will not play by these rules – I'll write a whole damn essay in the margins if I have to.

America, I speak to you not as a 'black man', but as an American. I am a patriot, just not the sort you're used to; my arguments today are in service to tomorrow. I serve unapologetically without obeying.

I have dreamed, as MLK once dreamed, of a better future; I have waited, and I have hoped. Yet my hopes have been dashed time and time again; I waited on the sidelines, hoping you would see reason. Hoping you would realize the abject folly of your ways, the flaws in the principles you stand on. The edifice of your empire may be carved by a thousand idealists, but it stands on shaking pillars

– your paradise is troubled, and a house of troubles cannot stand.

Like pieces of furniture, you gave us labels. The cruelest among these labels, the derogatory ones, were at least honest; they showed that you never considered us Americans to begin with. But now, you lacquer your words with sweeter sensibilities, pointing to us like a chair or table, labeled something absurd like "American Black – Newly Polished". You have objectified us and given us an identity with as much substance as a coat of varnish.

By giving us our 'race-name', you try to keep us exactly how you would love us to be: emasculated, powerless, and easy to control.

You teach us to be what you want us to be.

As a boy, I saw your lessons at work; I saw you abandon your people to their sins. You turned a blind eye to the yawning underbelly of your glittering cities, ignoring the moral decay and turpitude that crept through the streets like a knot of serpents. You watched as sin entered each home, as cold corruption seeped in and blew out

the hearths of love and family. Once, our communities had been tightly woven, aware of our identities – no more. Under your unloving eye, our houses became altars of alienation.

I lived in such a house, America. Like so many of us, I watched with wide eyes as men were replaced by hollow hedonists, as virtues were replaced by depravities. We, the forgotten, stood there in the dark shadow of your uncaring face, trying to drown out the sound of laughter and vice. You spoke of God in your rallies, spoke of His angels and His love; yet you abandoned His people. You betrayed us for a pittance of silver, and we stood between the Devil and the uncaring sea, with nowhere to turn to and no means of escape.

When I was younger, I was very unsure of myself. I lacked confidence in myself; my gaze was affixed outwards at everything but myself. I saw a whirlwind of chaos around me; even as I entered adulthood and grew less introverted, some traumas persisted. What I had lived through was not the American dream; it was a nightmare. Unsure and uncertain of my place in this country, I sought purpose. It took me many years, but I finally found it.

I am no longer the same uncertain and timid young Me'Shorn. It took age and a greying beard for me to finally become a dreamer again.

Uncle Sam, meet Uncle Me'Shorn.

***

To my readers: I address you directly now. If you have read so far, it is either in agreement or out of curiosity. Perhaps you wish to know me more, or perhaps you're waiting for me to substantiate my opinions and give my solution to the problems I have listed.

Now, at the age of 62, I have written this book to be as comprehensive as possible about all of these facets and more, so all questions will be answered in time. This book is the result of years of hope, despair, and everything in between – almost a lifetime of considerations and self- reflections. The alienation of my childhood gave me a fresh perspective, my youthful years gave me confidence, and age has given me insight. All of these have combined to make me who I am and make this book what it is.

Now I stand before you as a resolute champion for a better tomorrow. Perhaps I am simply too optimistic or naïve, but I still maintain hope in this country and always will.

This book is my truth, and I speak it for all to hear. There is much to discuss, much to talk about

– but it is best to begin at the beginning.

***

Beginnings are strange things.

Every end leads to a new beginning, and every beginning ends – like this very chapter. It's a constant; everything has to start somewhere. Almost everything has a point of origin, some point in the past it can be traced back to.

Whether it be a person, an object, a culture, or even an idea, everything in this material world has an origin – yet we have been alienated from ours. We knew that we, as a people, had an origin somewhere in the past, before the age of slavery.

Yet this past was distant and unreachable; now, we found ourselves following a thread through a shrouded maze, blundering and making fools of ourselves as we hope to reach our–

Roots.

*"Those who **respect** the elderly pave their own road toward **success**."*

African proverb.

It was 1977, and the miniseries Roots had just come out in a time when racism was at its peak. It was a spark that came at exactly the right time to resonate with its audience; in an instant, the spark had ignited a fire. Roots and the subsequent craze for it swept through the nation's 'black' communities like wildfire.

It was an impassioned, dangerous time. Our communities were high on reactionary fury, racial hyper-awareness, and vengeful wrath; we marched around, secure in our self-justifications. We were suddenly the chosen people, thinking of ourselves as the great oppressed; we were certain that any moral or social transgression we made was effectively nothing compared to what our ancestors and we had endured.

And so, full of flagrant, cocksure self- righteousness, we lost any claim to true righteousness. We became exactly what the construct told us to be – proud to be 'black'.

It was a renaissance of racial tensions. I remember it clearly: we all professed our hatred for 'whites' openly and often, taking pride in our capacity for hate. My mother had always hated white people, owing to certain experiences in her past. My father hated them too and caught up in this madness, so did I. We all did, men and women and children of all ages; young men all but spat on the sidewalk after mentioning "white people".
Even children in their schools looked down on any white kids they saw.

I remember how insane those days were. My friends and I wandered around like archetypical ruffians, itching for mischief, hateful of the very sight of white skin. And to my shame, I partook in this hatred to the extreme; I became one with the mob mentality that motivated the masses. It would take a long time before I realized my folly.

Although we didn't realize it, our hatred had reinforced the very stereotypes racists had cast us in: we had begun to act like hateful ruffians and criminals. We had played into their hands – we had become Their Black.

Why did this miniseries affect our community the way it did? Perhaps it would be helpful to explain what it was.

Roots was a miniseries based on a book called Roots: The Saga of an American Family. It followed the trials and tribulations faced by a Gambian man named Kunta Kinte, who is sold into slavery in North America, a supposed ancestor of the author, Alex Haley. Emphasizing the

cruelties of colonialism and racism, Haley had written a book
— and helped make a show — that connected the descendants of slaves to their ancient, pre-slavery past.

In essence, Haley had created a myth of greatness. In a parody of the biblical parable, Roots had made Africa synonymous with the garden of Eden; the "fall" of the "black man" from greatness was simply the biblical tale with racial themes shoe-horned in. But alienated victims of racism fell for it; we embraced the twisted parable with arms wide Open. We were convinced of our past greatness, convinced that we had been conned out of some heavenly land by the 'white devil'.

We were the descendants of slaves, wanting to escape to an earlier time. That is exactly what Roots offered: an origin and a glorious one at that. The idea was reinforced in 'black' churches, a phenomenon I luckily never partook in — even the iconography of Christ in these churches was suddenly amended to be 'black'. Even the spiritual had suddenly become subservient to material concerns such as color; something as common as the melanin in our skin had become the arbiter of morality and truth.

The stupidest — yes, the stupidest — part about this trend, however, was how flawed it was. It rested on the back of nostalgia without substance; it was an ahistorical mousetrap for the idealistic. As I matured in years, I decided to dig back into the roots of our conundrum — the real roots, historically documented.

Pre-colonial Africa, as it turns out, was home to at

least 800 distinct ethnic populations and cultures – in fact, that might well be a conservative figure, considering subcultures and groups within said ethnicities. These peoples and clans and kingdoms and tribes did never conform to a shared identity; they certainly didn't unite under a shared banner of 'blackness'. Without the concept of white, there was no concept of black; they were innocent of the skin-sins that dominate our age.

They were untainted by the color construct the European brought with him to Africa.

The Dark Continent, as it was known, was a place of riches, opportunities, and dangers for colonizers. They came to this mythical land, drawn like moths to flame, seeking wisdom, wealth, and power. The continent, at this time, was shaded and protected by venerable Elders; their wisdom and foresight prevented wars and clan feuds. These solemn, wise figures would protect their societies and peoples and act as moral arbiters and peacemakers. Even today, in many parts of Africa, respecting one's elders is a well-established cultural norm.

This culture of respect and understanding is what has been stripped away. This diversity of beliefs, values, and structures is what was lost. We didn't lose a single 'black' origin; we lost an entire paradigm, replaced by a corrupt European construct – a phenomenon that will be discussed in detail in Part II. But the point, again, is that what we lost in our past was complexity, not some mythical paradise. The tragedy is not that we lost our 'black origin' but that our many cultures were replaced by an obscene caricature called a black race.

'Black race'! Do you know the key difference between ethnicity and race? Here it is: an ethnicity considers the geographical and cultural identity of the people in question. But the very concept of race is based on physical characteristics, inspired by absurd and outdated concepts such as physiognomy. We, the descendants of slaves, are now without ethnicity – our many ethnicities were torn from us, replaced by the loathsome burden of race, the very burden we now cherish! Even sadder, we even try to be proud of this chain on our necks.

Now you tell me: is this not the damn stupidest thing?

Instead of acknowledging the trauma of our actual loss and remembering that we are the descendants of slaves torn from their wombs, we clamor for narratives of unity. Our communities crave a pre-slavery past, too embarrassed of our own ancestors! Led by demagogues and false prophets, the sons of slaves have forgotten their fathers, the fathers who no doubt cry crimson in their coffins. Remember us, they cry. Remember who you are.

What greater sacrilege can there be than to forsake your Elders? The slaves owned nothing but their words and left behind nothing but their memories – and now, so many of their sons have shed their legacies like a snake sheds its skin.

The search for identity has alienated them from their true selves; the search for roots has uprooted them; the search for a 'colored' God has made them Godless.

We aren't blacks. We aren't defined by our color, by the caricature of race slammed down on us by some

European oligarch too busy setting up plantations to bother to differentiate between the Igbo or Zulu or Maasai. To be proud of your 'blackness' is to be proud of a colonial remnant, a bitter gift from your oppressor.

But Uncle Me'Shorn, you cry. How else can I show that I'm proud of my forefathers and elders! Let me tell you: never forget where you came from. Never forget that you are descended from the slaves brought from their homeland 400-odd years ago, torn from their homes unceremoniously, mercilessly.

We are American Descendants of Slaves 1 – this is the only honest identity we can claim.
Everything else plays into the false narratives peddled by demagogues, hoping to drag others into their false narratives, their false promises. We can never – and should never – gloss over what our ancestors endured. Never forget the elders we have lost. Never forget the countless men and women who suffered in silence. Never forget the chains, for they still bind us, if only with a shred of subtlety now.

Look closer – this country's institutions and narratives are our manacles, our padlock and chain, our iron gibbet. Every reality of slavery we claim to have left in the past still lives – every claim to have become assimilated into a new, normalized America is false. We may be Americans in our hearts, but America has never accepted us; to claim us otherwise is wishful thinking. They represent us in their media, pay homage to our musical talent, and make quotas and spaces for us, but we remain 'the blacks' to them. We find ourselves relegated to roles in entertainment industries, unable to flourish anywhere else because they keep Their Black caged in quotas. We stay here as internal exiles, and the only way forward is to first accept this fact.

To all those who grew up believing in a fair and just America, believing they had any right in this country, my sincerest apologies: I know the pain of finding out the truth so bluntly. I'd soften the blow if I could – but those in service to truth cannot mince words.

We must first unlearn to then relearn.

To explain what that means, let me tell you a story I once heard about the Buddha. They say that a milk-man once offered the Buddha fresh milk if he came to his house and gave him some
wisdom. The Buddha agreed and went to his house with a bowl, intentionally putting some dirt in it.

The milk-man removed the dirt from the bowl before pouring in the milk; after having a drink, the Buddha made as if to leave.

"Wait," cried the milk-man. "Where is the wisdom you promised me?"

He had already given it, explained the Buddha.
To pour milk into the bowl, it was necessary to first remove the dirt. It was simple: to accept anything good into the vessel, one must remove that which is bad from within it.

Unless you can first unlearn that which is wrong, anything new you learn will be polluted by your prior understanding. Therefore, it is necessary to relearn things from scratch; when you set out in the search for truth, abandon all prior assumptions. Abandon the Factualism embedded in your mind. Abandon the thousand coping mechanisms you have constructed. Abandon the corrupted self that has justified inequity for so long – lose yourself in the pursuit of truth.

Not too long ago, I was conversing with a young man who was telling me how the Pharaohs were 'black'. I asked him a simple thing: were these pharaohs good folk or bad? He looked at me blankly and asked me why that mattered – why that mattered! It surely mattered more than the melanin in their skin; surely, the measure of a man is more than just whether he was 'black' or not. We have become so caught up, so ensnared by color, that we can't see nothing else.

To make myself perfectly clear, I don't mean to say that the past doesn't matter – I mean to say that the past matters too much to be reduced to a petty slogan. As Descendants, we are connected not to obscure kings and theoretical notions of a racial utopia but to the real men and women who lived, suffered, and died on American soil. They are our ancestors, our Elders – they are our direct link to our identity, that fickle, flighty thing we chase around like blind men.

Our true selves can only be rediscovered by reconnecting with the fallen, understanding their message and learning from their lives and struggles. We cannot allow them to fade into the abyss. They say a man dies two deaths: once when he dies and again when he is forgotten. It is our responsibility that our forefathers never die this second death and continue to live in our actions.

　　Our roots will always define us – they surely define me. If you wish to know a man, always learn what he has been through and the choices he made; that's a nugget of wisdom from your Uncle Me'Shorn. If you wish to know me, here's what you need to know about–

Footnotes For Roots Chapter

1 American Descendants Of Slaves Ethnic Identity "American Descendants of
Slaves" instead of Racial Identity: " Black"As long as we don't define ourselves based on a reality that connects us to our ancestors, we will be stuck in the pigeonhole of being "America's Black", Durante Vita! Durante Vita - This is a Latin term that means "during life". This is the term the Maryland Assembly used when describing the duration of slavery for "Negroes" or "People of African descent" back in 1664. Before this nation was the nation it is today the government of the day deemed "black people" would be relegated to being slaves from birth until death... Durante Vita.

In the present time, we live in an age of self-identification. This is especially the case when it comes to gender. Born males can identify as "she" or "her" and born females can identify as "he" or "him" and society goes along with this. Fine.

Self-identification has been acceptable, but not when it comes to "race". If you are "black" you can't wake up one day and decide to be "white", even though through skin bleaching many have tried. Not even Albinism can change a "black person", to "white". What we can do is reject racial identification and identify as who we truly are. That is the logic behind the term "American Descendants of Slaves" (for those of us within the African Diaspora that this ethnic identity applies to). If society "allows" people to pick and choose their pronouns, why does our government have such a difficult time accepting the ethnic identity "American Descendants of Slaves"?!Why do the powers that be, continue to insist on relegating us to "black" or whatever pigeonhole they have prepared for us? Worse, why do we allow "them" to define who we are based on their definition of who "we" are?

(Contributed by Leonard E. Walker)

Who I Am.

> "**Roots** are not in landscape or a country, or a people; they are **inside you**."
>
> Isabel Allende.

When you ask me, Who are you, Uncle Me'Shorn? You're actually asking me, Where did you come from, Uncle Me'Shorn?

Let me tell you that all origins are myths – they can be true, or they can be false. The moment I was born, I entered into a reality shaped by myths. To look into the roots of my myth, we have to first look at my maternal grandparents.

***

When I first saw a picture of my granddaddy, I couldn't recognize him.

That's no surprise, you think; surely, it'd be hard to recognize your grandfather when you've never met the man.

But no, that isn't the reason why I couldn't recognize him – the problem was that he looked too 'white'!

Now, Lewis Congus Conley – that was his name – had his own problems. Chief among them was that he knew he looked too white; he didn't look dark enough to pass for 'his own'. What my granddaddy carried in his heart was a shame, and it was a shame for something he'd never done. Life never asked him what color skin he wanted; he never consented to be born light-skinned, but there he was, sticking out like a sore thumb in his times. He was just white enough to pass for white but not white enough to be comfortable with it.

And so, what drew him to my grandmother wasn't love. Most weddings at the time weren't decided on the basis of love, but in his case, it was especially obvious: he was only marrying Hattie Peebles for her tar-black skin. She was coal dark, as 'black' as you can imagine – and the symbolic value of that color is what attracted Louis Conley to ask for her hand. He'd always be the man who looked whiter than he was – but his children would have a better fate. They'd fit in because they'd be 'proper black'.

My grandparents worked for a family called the Nelsons. It was as colonial a background as you can imagine; she was a maid for them, while he was a caretaker for their facilities. My mother was named Hattie Laura Conley, and she was the second-youngest out of nine siblings.

In later life, her carelessness would bring me to much grief – and though there is much I blame her for, I also understand why she was never the most stable woman.

From the moment of her birth, she saw the colonial

society that had shaped my grandparents. She had been born at the behest of a man who simply wished to have children to wash away the shame of his apparent 'whiteness'.

She once told me a story – one that her mother had told her in her childhood. Back when my grandmother was young – sometime in the 1920s

– their lawful property had been stolen from them by white people. But not only did they steal the property, but according to her, they burnt it down out of sheer spite.

This story was passed on from my grandmother to my mother, who then passed it to me. These were her roots, the very roots she passed onto me.

Then there was my birth-father.

His name was Clyde Me'Shorn Floyd, and that name came from his grandmother – my paternal great-grandmother. She named him Me'Shorn for reasons that were her own, and she named him Clyde after the French owner of Clydesdale Horses and Slaves.

As the two got married, my mother was almost twenty years old. In only a short time, she got pregnant, and soon after, she had a child.

Yes, this child was yours truly: Uncle Me'Shorn.

***

I was born on the 6th of January, 1961, on Epiphany

day – the significance of which I've pondered on for much of my life, which I'll discuss later on.

In any case, on that day in Miami, Florida, a tiny infant came into this world in the maternity ward of Jackson Memorial Hospital. There I was, little Me'Shorn, as sweet and innocent as any baby might be – but as a clever fellow named Descartes put it: Man is born free, but everywhere he is in chains. Scarce had I uttered my first cry since exiting the womb, that I was already bound to the fated happenstance of history, destined to be a new link in a familial chain.

It's a funny thing, the miracle of birth. I was born against my will; man doesn't get consulted about nothing in the circumstances of his existence. You get born without your consent, named without your consent, and raised without your consent.

For your whole life, you're tagged with a name you never got to choose – yet your name still defines you. It bleeds into your upbringing and colors your childhood. You try to escape it or live up to it, learn to accept it or revile it – but names stick. You can change a hundred if you like, passing through them like seasonal coats, but you're stuck with your given name. It will always be a part of you, whether you like it or not.

You may have noticed that Me'Shorn wasn't my father's first name, nor was it his last name, so it need not have passed down to me – thinking about it one day, I asked my mother why she gave me his name. What she told me was nothing short of terrible. My father, the man responsible for a whole half of my being, hadn't wished for me to be born! He had wanted her to abort me; my mother gave me his middle name to stop him from abandoning me.

Apparently, it was enough to save my life but not enough to keep him from leaving us.

So you see, even as a newborn, I was never a clean slate. My being, my psyche, and my traumas were predestined from the moment of my conception – it was not my fault my birth-father didn't want me, but I paid for it nonetheless. I never asked to be Me'Shorn, but that is who I became.

When I was a young child, I was tongue-tied and socially clumsy. Certain events in my childhood (that I shall discuss later in this book) left me as a quiet and troubled boy. I had just gotten over the hellish prospect of mingling with other children, and I had done surprisingly well, I thought. I was talking to others, and things seemed to be going well.

Yet my name ended up hindering my gingerly attempts at normalizing my life. The worst episode occurred at roll call at one point.

I noticed that my teacher was deliberately messing up my name by mispronouncing it. This wasn't the first time I had been through this exhausting song and dance; I had faced a similarly sadistic teacher during my kindergarten years.

In this particular instance, I remember this teacher calling out the names of my classmates, marking their presence. By now, I knew that she couldn't pronounce my name; when it came up, she stopped abruptly, struggling to pronounce it. Giving up, she spoke at the top of her voice:

"Is there a Mess-Horn in this class?"

"Yes, ma'am," I said, wincing as I raised my hand. This time, I scared up the nerve to correct her. "My name is Me'Shorn. M-E-S-H-O-R-N."

I held my breath, hoping it would end there. It didn't.

That teacher responded, "And my name is Me-Teacher!"

And then, the class burst into mad fits of laughter, and my face burned with embarrassment. Soon after, my classmates began teasing me incessantly. So where was the fault?

Was it mine? Was it my name's?

Mortified by the instance and the resulting surge of teasing, bullying, and harassment it caused, I went through one of the worst things a child could go through: I started hating my own name. I started to despise the syllables of it, hated how it wasn't normal, hated everything it stood for. Hate is a poison, a cancer, and for many years, it poisoned the wells of my heart.

It took years to heal from this self-hate. Today I am a man of love, only because I made peace with my name. I made peace with myself. I accepted my roots, my inheritance, without shame.

***

To leave the loop of hatred is a daunting task. There were many people, ideologies,

paradigms, institutions, and phases of life that I had grown to hate in my youth. It was a difficult childhood for many reasons – it embittered my young heart, and my passions were inflamed to the point of approaching a wildfire. I still remember snapping at my mother at one point; she had grown so used to me being a quiet roll-over, willing to take any abuse, that she felt no reticence while doling out. But finally, enough was enough – I remember standing up for myself and yelling back at her.

It wasn't altogether out of hatred that I reacted; I had repressed myself for so long that it was inevitable that I would explode. Yet this is the trap of hatred; it emboldens your heart while poisoning it from the inside.

Having been born in 1961, I still remember the period of racism – back when a good part of the American public still didn't care that the segregation laws had been repealed. I remember walking through the city streets, in restaurants and diners, seeing areas labeled "White Only". My mother explained to me that these areas were forbidden to me – they were only for 'the whites'. Unaware of the color-construct that drove everything around me, I reacted as any child would – at first, I wondered; then I protested; and then I grew bitter.

Later, as me and my youthful friends spoke ill of white people, we spoke without reservation. At that moment, we became the prime example of the most dangerous part of hate: we began to 'Other' the whites. We became convinced they were a faceless enemy. We fell into a 'Us vs. Them' psychology, where we were the good guys, and they were our stereotypical evil oppressors. They could do no right. We could do no wrong.

Then how did I break free? How did I learn to give up on this hate?

For one thing, I had never become a part of the 'black churches' in the country. For reasons of her own, my mother had never let us attend; thus, even though my hate burned strongly, it was not nearly as strong as many others who were my age. My most impressionable years had certainly been traumatic, but they were comparatively less full of narratives and indoctrination. The tragedies of my childhood had, in a sense, kept me distracted from the wider propaganda-paradigm that continued to create divisions between people, reinforcing racial hatred.

But a big help for me in shedding the hate-shackles society had put on me was critical thinking. I could examine a thing from all angles, asking questions that no one else had bothered to ask. When you're a child, you ask the most inane questions: Why is the sky blue? How do birds fly? Yet, at some point, something kills off this curiosity and makes you another mundane schmuck willing to go through life without ever looking up. You lose the ability to ask the most obvious questions – you lose the ability to analyze your own life and learn the lessons that it teaches.

Go look in the mirror. Take a hard look – remember your past and how it's shaped you. Remember the details, the memories, the big events – now ask yourself why they happened.

One day, as a full-grown man, I sat in my room and thought about why my mama encouraged me to enroll in the army. What did she see back then?

What was she thinking? If I hadn't had that experience, would I be the Me'Shorn that I am today?

Sure, you can call this type of thinking unproductive – but not everything has to be immediately productive, damn it! Ask the 'stupid' questions that no one expects you to ask. And most importantly, ask the uncomfortable questions – the ones people don't like you asking.

Ask yourself why so many figures in this country claiming to stand for 'love' keep talking in the most hate-mongering manner. Ask yourself why the people who talk so strongly against racism talk about hate and color and race the most. Ask yourself why this country is content to sweep that whole conversation under the rug.

Question the narratives around you. Question the obvious truth – because Uncle Me'Shorn can assure you someone paid a lot of money to make it seem like the obvious truth!

The only way to enter love is to find the narratives that promote hate; distance yourself from them, and reject the hate-construct.

In the end, all that you need to know about who I am is this: I am my beginnings, and I am my choices. As I realized this, like a baby out of the incubator, I began to find myself– and I found this self in a place called the "Little Black Book", by Norris Shelton. The contents of this book made me look within, unto my own identity.

I realized the history of my people in that book.

A people with many names, yet those names demonstrate a keen lack of knowledge. Upon landing on the shores of North America, we were Black Slaves, then just Slaves, then Niggers, then griffes, then quadroons, then Mualottos, then Octoroons, then Negroes, then Black.

But identifying oneself as these is to lose who you are and become who they say you are. And this is why I chose the name 'African American'. Being an African American it connects you to your origin. Your character is developed based on your name; You act as you believe you are. If you live under the black identity, that is who you will ever be.

But Me'Shorn T. Daniels had evolved from all of these so-called names. The evolution of a man is not an easy feat when you are born out of misery and thrust upon a land that is not your own; but that identification has empowered me. It is why I strive to be all I can be, and I have faith that one day we will all get there. The aggressiveness within me is the hunger of freedom that we all should have; I have evolved into my purpose. Who I am is not static; it has been a process of becoming, and now I have become the Me'Shorn I was always meant to be.

My origins, my roots, tether me in place. They are my unshakeable center, the pivot of my soul – they anchor me and keep me who I am. I am an American Descendant of Slaves; I am the scared child who went through so much; and I am the army-man who did his best for this country. I am connected to each facet of my past in a way that is impossible to break. There is nothing fluid, flexible, or transient in my connection to my roots – they run as strong and powerful as the roots of oak trees, deep under the earth.

But my choices have brought me life. My choice to reject hate changed my life; my choice to question everything around me enriched me. It's why sullen and angry little Me'Shorn grew into Uncle Me'Shorn. It's why I can stand before you today, proud of Who I Am.

***

Make no mistake; it's a slippery thing to pin down exactly Who You Are.

We spend our entire lives being ourselves but without a clue about our true selves. Things are even more complicated when this self lies mired under years of experiences, traumas, and desires; it's covered in so many layers of borrowed identity that knowing Who You Are becomes a damn chore.

We think we are who we believe ourselves to be, or whatever our job or vocation is – some of the young folk out there even define themselves based on sexuality, of all things. Nowadays, it's a whole trend to think that our identities are in our own hands. That we have the choice in the matter of who we like to be, as though our true self is externally re-writable.

But that isn't how this works. I am who I am because I was born as I was, I was raised as I was, and I learned the things that I did.

Our personal self originates much earlier than what most of us believe; it can all be traced back to our –

Early Years.

*"It is easier to **build** strong children than to **repair** brokenadults."*

Fredrick Douglass.

We all begin with our parents.

On the template of Adam and Eve, man and woman create life; this life grows to become a person in their own right, like me or you. Our soul may begin with God, but our self begins with our parents – we are shaped by being born and brought up. We rise from the metaphorical sea, like land, but the sea continues to shape us; the waves batter away at the shores of our being until we become what we are.

In a sense, growing is not only a pattern of creation. It is not an eternal list of added value – often, our youths consist of losing things. We lose our inquisitiveness, our innocence, and our naivety. Instead of growing in a straight line, we continuously gain and lose aspects of ourselves, whether by accident or purpose. The influences of our parents and the society around us mold us like clay; they edit the essential truth of who we are, cutting parts away or adding new ones. Our subconscious is battered and buffed like a car getting fixed, beaten into shape like an iron ingot.

In this way, just as God created the essential Fact of you, your parents attempted to remake you in their own image or according to their aspirations. When these aspirations are noble, they develop a child's mind and character, teach them morality, and make them a better person.

Primary socialization occurs at this stage, and children learn norms and values from their parents. However, if the parent is absent, uncaring, or simply dysfunctional in their approach to parenting, the result is maladjusted children who can have their entire futures ruined.

This is not to say that a child who has gone through the most terrible upbringing is forced to live and die within that flawed or perverse paradigm – after all, I myself suffered through a largely abusive childhood. It is completely possible to make the conscious choice to push past the traumas you have endured, and learn to make a path for yourself that defies the unnatural actions of your parents.

However, there is a question I sometimes ponder in the dead of night when everyone else sleeps. I find myself wondering about those who are never able to leave the horrific teachings of their parents. I wonder about those who never had the required revelation; I wonder about those who still carry idols of their false fathers, confusing the devil with the saint. How many of these children grow up to be deeply flawed men and women?

How many of them suffer deep scars that make them depressed, unreasonable, and even harmful to others? Go get on a subway, and on the opposite seats, you'll most likely find yourself looking at a lineup of broken people.

Half of who we are is already decided in our early years. People assume that infants simply lose all their memories as they grow up, but that's not true. Even if we do not consciously remember

certain memories, they persist in our subconscious; nothing is ever truly forgotten. Nothing is ever truly lost. As Freud might have put it, we're constantly in the process of repressing our past memories, trying to hide the traumas that made us.

Our early years are especially poignant because this is when we are utterly helpless. Unlike horses, we don't fall from the womb ready to run circles around a fence; we come into this world naked and helpless. Even an infant's head is too large for it to support! Our state of utter vulnerability means that as a whole species, we depend on our parents for food, warmth, and shelter; we depend on their skills, knowledge, morality, and emotional concern. Life itself rests on the sheer, blind trust an infant has for its parents.

The parent, therefore, is equivalent to a god for a child. The child thus sees their mother and father as parent-gods, the absolute origins and arbiters of identity and morality. They are the center around which the child orbits, warming it like the sun does the earth. By having children, an individual knowingly or unknowingly enters into the role of being a parent-god; it is an arch-responsibility, a burden that must be carried with the greatest solemnity. Everything that is human begins with parenting.

Yet parent-gods, unlike God above, can be flawed. They can fall into temptation and sin; they can lose their path or forget their responsibilities. And though a parent's love is ideally unconditional, this is not always the case; some never love their children, some put conditions on their affection, and some monsters are happy to abuse their children. To occupy a divine seat is a task for which many humans are unfit; they are too caught up in their mortal sins to aspire to anything beyond.

When parent-gods fall, they take their children with them. This is the root of familial dysfunction; this is where the sin of the father tries to corrupt the child. Dysfunction in the individual is rooted in a dysfunctional family experience during one's early years. The early years of our lives can strongly impact the rest of it – and if you need an example, I can do better than quote case studies. I can tell you what I have been through.

***

As I mentioned earlier, my mother was around twenty when I was born. Soon after her divorce, she had to start working and earning a wage to provide for herself and her kid – me.

Yet that begged the question, who would take care of me? We clearly weren't loaded enough with cash to afford to get a professional babysitter or nanny. What she needed was a relative who could care for me while she was away working.

Now, I obviously don't blame her for having to work at that stage; nor do I blame her for getting help raising me. But unfortunately, she made her choice with a clear display of ill-judgment.

He was known in the family as Uncle Solomon, though he wasn't strictly my uncle – he was my grandfather's brother. Now this man was well known to be an alcoholic; hardly the best candidate to care for an infant. But either this detail escaped my mother's memory, or she simply didn't know; in either case, the final result was that she gave me over to this drunkard while she herself would leave for work.

She'd learn only much later that he'd been molesting me.

Infantile memories generally don't stay for most people, but I remember some memories with unfortunate clarity; the trauma is burnt into my mind. Hell, I even remember an instance of this Uncle Solomon molesting me. I remember the nauseating, horrible sensation of it. The thought of it still sickens me; even now, I ask myself, what sort of man would do that to a child? What sort of human? Even so little, I knew something wrong or bad was happening to me. Even then, I knew something unnatural was occurring – something wrong.

I don't know why I need to even say this, but you don't need somebody to tell you that sexual assault is wrong. Even in a state of complete innocence, a child knows when something wrong is being done to it.

The experience of being molested by Uncle Solomon, a 'man' from my own family, was enough to crush me. Even full-grown adults go into shock if sexually assaulted; I was only a child. The idol of the parent-god in my head immediately shattered – it was torn asunder by the barbarity of this disgusting event. It was an event as destructive as any. And as I grew, I continued to suffer from it.

As I mentioned, I grew up to be a quiet kid. My early childhood, in fact, passed almost stone- mute; I was normal in all aspects, but I refused to talk. My mother took me from psychiatrist to psychiatrist, hoping to coax me out of my shell; and when I did finally start to emerge, bullying in school added another layer of misery to my life.

Yet 'Uncle Solomon' wasn't the only cause of my trauma. Despite all her attempts to give me a good life, my mother continued to make wrong decisions.

It's a strange happenstance that throughout my life, I have had three fathers: the first was my birth-father, who left us without a care. The third was my foster-father, a man who was perhaps the most duplicitous of them all.

Between these two, the second was my almost-father, someone she met when I was young. His name was Joey, and as I would later learn, he was a pimp. I was quiet but quick to observe; my keen eye and memory have kept these incidents disconcertingly sharp in my mind.

Joey was always surrounded by women whom he was none-too-kind with. He was nice enough to my mother, but he didn't hesitate to cuss at the other women who accompanied or met him.

One day, I asked him why he talked to them like that. He never answered the question, but he did reassure me he'd never talk to my mother like that – because she was 'his'. I was surprised; the implication of her 'belonging' to him was a bizarre notion, one that made little sense to a young child.

I wondered how a person could belong to someone else.

I remember when I accompanied my mother in the car as she went over to pick Joey up. As always, he met her surrounded by ladies. It soon became evident that his female friends didn't like my mom; he clearly treated her far more nicely compared with the rest of them. I still remember her tears as she cried later from their jabs and jeers. In that moment, she had feared for her life.

What child would forget seeing his mother like that?
Soon after, Joey disappeared from her life. He was replaced by a man my mother introduced as responsible and respectable. He was also a police officer.

This man was destined to be my third father.

Together, we moved into a new city and neighborhood. For once, things seemed to be going well; it seemed like she had finally found a good man to live her life with. He provided us with everything he could, and we were happy and satisfied. Life was beginning to become more stable, and I began to indulge in that luxury called 'hope'. Perhaps, I thought, things could become better after all.

My hope was misplaced. Things never stayed stable for long in my life, and that was about to be the case yet again.

It was midnight when I was awoken by the sound of loud voices coming from my parents' room. I crept there, scared and confused; as I neared the room, I realized they were in a heated argument. I had no clue what they were fighting about.

But I remember vividly that my father was no longer my father the next morning at the breakfast table. My mother talked to him in such a manner that even I was shocked. My mother, who had placed him on a pedestal herself, was suddenly disrespecting him. The way she bellowed and screamed at him scared me.

My mother had presented my father as the best person ever; now here I was, watching this scene unfold before me. He didn't seem to like her behavior either; I looked at them both, confused and hurt. He was the only one whom I had ever respected – like I would have done to my real father.

The irony was that instead of disliking him, I started disliking my mother. Some may judge me for it, but as a child, it felt justified to me; this man had been doing his best to be a good father to me up until now. He gave me everything a real father would have given his children; he spent time with me, took me fishing, and gave me care and attention – things I was starved for.

But from that terrible morning at the breakfast table, the man I considered to be my father changed utterly. His entire demeanor changed; gone was the man I thought of as closer to me than my own blood-father. Gone were the fishing trips, the time together, the care and attention. All his efforts to be likable to me ceased. Worse yet, he started calling me names. He'd abuse my biological father around me, picking on me over all sorts of things. Before I could even process what had happened, the entire relationship dynamic had been swept out from under me; in a single night, I had gone from being his son to a nuisance he seemed to barely tolerate.

I hated it.

But I stayed silent, tolerating everything for my mother's sake. Whether or not the fault was hers, he was still her husband, and I had no idea what had even prompted this sudden change. Anxious, miserable, and scared of every possible misstep that might annoy him, I grew up in the presence of perpetual fear. This state of affairs carried on into my teens.

All of these events scarred me. Growing up with my family was not like the linear growth most other kids seemed to enjoy; mine was a one-step- forward, two-steps-back sort of childhood. For every moment of growth, I'd face a new trauma that would lead to a fresh state of regression.

Helpless, I'd open and shut like a window in a cyclone; the worst horror was that persistent little spark of hope that existed only to warm me between bouts of sharp pain and disappointment.

Between being picked on at home and being bullied in school, my childhood did no wonders for my self-esteem – in fact, I now think I barely had one. A child is helpless by nature; children cannot exercise their will over the world around them, and they certainly cannot hope to create a 'self' without the help of the Parent-God, the divine

vice-sergeant that governs the life of a youth. Yet my Parent-Gods were false idols; their teachings came as storms and undeserved penance.

And so, from the very beginning of myself, I came from storms. There was a storm outside of me, which were the circumstances I have described – and then there was the storm inside of me. My emotions were knotted up within me with no way out, and they crashed against my soul like tides against the shore. Young Me'Shorn was a scarred little boy, alone in torment.

***

As bleak as it is, the structure of my early life is a part of a bigger structure. This structure is what I described earlier as Who I Am; it is the structure that defines my very self- identity.

Yet all structures have forms that are supported by frameworks. The framework keeps the structure aloft; the structure defines us, and the framework defines the structure. This framework is like the scaffolding around a large project – and simultaneously, it is also like the wire mesh around which the structure is built.

When it comes to human lives, this framework is two-sided. On the one hand is the obvious: context. I have described this aspect of the framework so far by recounting my early life, my roots, and the times I grew up in – however, the second part of the framework is arguably even more vital. But what could be more vital than context?

The answer is this: Events that are too vital, too powerful to be called context. These are events that aren't just background noise or a general haze of events that inform an individual's growth; these aren't just events that you have experienced, but rather, they are events that have changed your entire experience of existence.

If the structures of our lives are like

human bodies, it's apt to call these

frameworks–

Skeletons.

*"But in life, we don't usually get to choose the time of our defining moments. We just have to **stand** and **face** them whenthey come, no matter what sort of a state we're in."*

Darren Shan.

Skeletons in the closet.

You've probably heard the phrase – its bandied around pretty regularly, carrying the implication of something shameful or unwholesome hidden away by an individual who wants to be distanced from it.

But we all have our skeletons, and they all define us – whether they're strung out in the 'closet' or not is immaterial. The skeleton is the most important part of the human anatomy; the skeletons in our life are likewise vital frameworks for the rest of us. Perhaps the terminology occurs to me because I am in the surgical profession. It's a strange thought, but most of my work as a surgical technologist over the past forty years boils down to catering to things that are defined, shaped, or housed by the human skeleton. The skeletons I refer to now are not dissimilar; our lives are defined, shaped, and interred within these skeletons.

Be they events, memories, or traumas, we can never live a life free of them – even if we wish to bury them. For years, I tried to rid myself of the skeletons that haunt me, facelessly grinning phantoms of the past, the unforgettable images burnt into my mind.

But we cannot escape.

***

So, instead of running from them, let us talk about my skeletons.

I already mentioned one of these: that is to say, me being molested by a family member as an infant. Uncle Solomon is my first skeleton, the first one I encountered. Even in the cradle, this skeleton was horrific enough to change my entire life – due to it, my conception of the parent-god was irrevocably tarnished, nullified. I was lost like a planet out of orbit like the earth sent hurtling through space with the disappearance of the sun – my anchor had been uprooted.

Sexual assault, even when faced at such a young age, can have an adverse impact on future relationships. When abused children get into adult romantic relationships, they often fall prey to depression or anxiety and lose their sense of self-respect. They may even cease to have any sexual desires or, conversely, get a high sexual drive.

But no matter the overall impact of the act, one thing is for certain: there's no going back.

This is the key thing about skeletons in general

– they do not allow a return. They do not allow you to sample some trauma, heal, and return to a place of blissful ignorance. You can unlearn but you can never undo. You can change your conception of the past, but never the past itself; you can change your way of dealing with or seeing the skeleton, but you can never get rid of its rattling bones. The skeleton wants to be heard – it wants to be remembered. Leave the skeleton in the closet, and you'll find yourself lying awake at night, thinking of nothing but the closet and its contents.

Repression is a natural response to trauma, but is it really the right answer in the long term? No.
We must confront our skeletons and accept their existence. The only way to move past is to not turn back.

***

The next skeleton in my life was my parents – or, more specifically, my Mother.

Growing up, my mother took the place reserved for god. Even though the illusion of the parent-god had shattered for me in principle, in practice, she continued to play the role; even though my mind could not revolve around her with the same heartwarming awe other children hold for their mothers, I continued to physically depend on her. This complicated my feelings greatly, because even though I was mentally distanced from her often, this could not be reflected materially.

My mother played the parent-god, but the role she

played was not the natural one. The parent-god is meant to be God's viceroy in the child's life, the physical manifestation of God's love for the infant. By sheltering, caring for, and generally working to their child's benefit, the parent assumes the mantle of pseudo-divinity, but only in God's name – like a religious cross or ornament, which isn't holy itself, but assumes a religious gravity because of what it represents.

My mother, on the other hand, was the sole monarch in her sphere of influence – namely, me. Little Me'Shorn was growing up in a world without God; even though it was for the best that I grew up without the presence of black churches in my life, I was very much sheltered from the very concept of God. It would take years before I found Him.

So there was no divine authority behind the lone parent-god that controlled my life – and the godless king has no option but tyranny. You can quote your Uncle Me'Shorn on that.

In short, she played the dominant matriarch, the arbiter of just and unjust, and the ultimate authority behind all things. She interjected into my life when needed and remained alien from it whenever she wanted. Her presence was simultaneously intangible and oppressive, ephemeral and inescapable; you couldn't escape from her if you tried, but she was nowhere to be found when she was truly needed.

Do I blame her? Not entirely: she was a lone woman, doing her best.

But bigger mistakes were being made.

***

The next skeleton is also connected, in part, to my mother. This skeleton was, in fact, a series of events – the traumatic examples of open sexuality during my childhood.

After my mom married my foster father, I would later learn that they were less than normal in their sexual exploits. They were embroiled in what can only be called an open relationship, but even that would imply a certain degree of method to their madness. But no, it was as openly immoral as you could imagine; they were particularly interested in swapping partners. My mother took no great pains to shelter my sister and me from this sexual openness – on the contrary, she was very upfront about explaining it to us.

Living in this over-sexed, dysfunctional environment, things were quite complicated. They'd be fighting and arguing one minute and indulging in something unspeakable the next. It was hardly any atmosphere to raise children in, but that certainly didn't stop them.

There is no way for developing children to live in this sort of atmosphere without being profoundly affected by it – and the effects this childhood had on us shame me to this very day.

My parents often left my sister and me alone at home. So my sister (who will remain nameless here) and I used to be alone at home. We'd set the house up by ourselves, play and watch movies, read books, and scatter toys all over the floor as most children do. Closing my eyes, I can still see the multicolored toys spread all over our mattresses – but it's never a happy memory.

Amid these innocent toys, we began to demonstrate symptoms of our very twisted upbringing. We were influenced by things we didn't understand – and my mother's negligence was beginning to show its horrific impact on her children's lives. Emulating my mother, we began to play a game.

It was called 'Mommy and Daddy'.

Even recounting it shames me, but this is a skeleton I must confront. Though I would love to turn away and never think about it again, we can never go back – there is never any escape from the past. And though I will never escape the shame that still smothers my heart, it burns even more that we had our innocence and sexuality stolen from us because of our parents.

Once corrupted even slightly, innocence is a thing that destroys itself completely. We made the most innocuous of plans, yet we'd end up doing things we shouldn't have. Soon, we realized what we were doing was wrong – but this was the irony. We were too innocent to know exactly how wrong it was. To us, it was wrong like breaking a vase is wrong; it was wrong like any other childish misdeed is wrong. Once sullied by our mother's negligence, our innocence self-immolated, and we were left in the painful, horrific shame of our deeds, like the dysfunctional shame of Adam and Eve when they sinned and fell in the biblical narrative.

I can even partially justify some of my mother's neglect as her being too busy to notice. But that isn't all – her part in the premature debasement of our sexuality was active. Not only did she (very vividly) discuss the sexual nature of her relationship with her husband, she did something worse: she allowed her own children to become embroiled in this sexual mess.

To put it starkly, she allowed her own daughter to have a sexual relationship with her husband.

Now, my sister was not genetically related to our foster father, but I hardly need to explain why I consider this relationship to be perverse and incestuous. The 'games' my sister and I had indulged in were bad enough, but they stemmed from youthful ignorance and a desire to emulate the adults around us. However, this extramarital, fetishized relationship between my sister and our foster father was completely unnatural, motivated by a man's lust for a girl he should have cared for as his daughter.

By this point, I was a young teen, and I was becoming uncomfortably aware of how wrong our familial situation was. When I was among our friends, they often talked about their lives. I'd stand there, tongue-tied, listening to them in silence. Obviously, I could not talk about my dysfunctional childhood with people of my age. As they talked, I discovered their childhoods to be ripe with innocence.

Suddenly, I realized just how different I was from them.

But since I couldn't utter a word, I withdrew into my

shell instead. I'd go home afterward, sitting on my bed, dissociated – I realized how wrong my life was. I realized how wrong my family was. There was something unhealthy and destructive about them, something that was willing to consume and ruin us all.

To this day, I carry the mental trauma of the 'liberated' childhood I lived through. I pray that no one else have to live through something like it again.

***

Skeletons aren't just baggage.

They define you, and in many cases, they lead to the formation of even more skeletons. The framework self-replicates; it grows and evolves, creating self from self.

In this way, the previous skeletons also led to a new one – sexual alienation. In the wake of the horrible things I had faced as a child, the natural sexuality I would have evolved was instead dysfunctional and stunted; in fact, aside from my experiences with my sister, I had no experience in sexual relationships. I knew some things – of course, it was hard not to in my family – but overall, I still retained a distance to sex that was not quite average for younger men.

I grew keenly aware of this when I joined the military. Men around me were generally very sexually active, to the point where I felt consciously alienated. Furthermore, many of these fellows might have been sexually mature, but they sure as all hell weren't mature in any other sense; they were happy to ridicule me for being different, for being so detached from the vagaries of lust that most young men spend their days in.

The first time I was in a real, legitimate sexual relationship was as an adult, and even then, a keen part of her interest in me was because of how different I was from other men.

In some ways, it was the same as school – I watched silently as I again found myself alienated and ostracized yet again.

***

As you can see, Uncle Me'Shorn was not always the man you see before you today. I've struggled with my skeletons, and even though I regret many things I have been through and done, I still feel proud to have made my way past them. In fact, without these skeletons, your Uncle Me'Shorn, the man I am today, would not exist.

By sharing these skeletons with you, I want my readers to understand that it is through these challenges that we grow stronger and more robust. A broken bone heals twice as hard; a torn muscle renews itself twice as tough.

The skeletons that were the realities of my life nearly destroyed me. I hit rock bottom, in a state of absolute loathing, having lost my natural innocence and vitality. But I learned through these tribulations how these challenges define us. This mindset, the ability to face our skeletons, separates us from the people who succumb to these challenges and give up or hide them away under a false veneer of smiles and cologne. Had I done the same thing, I would never have been the person I am today; I would be another broken, maladjusted human being.

Thus, we may all face challenges and obstacles, but the main thing is to move past them. It is never a straight road to our dreams and ambitions, but you must first make peace with your skeletons before all else.

When we are at the lowest points in our lives, that's when we truly begin to become. In that crucible, we are faced with choices, and presented with the opportunity to make a powerful decision. Life can show you many roads, but it is up to you to push and motivate yourself to move to a better place.

Remember, you are the only person who can use your lowest moments to your advantage.

Whenever I think back to my early years, I remember a saying; "You can't connect the dots looking forward; you can only connect them looking backwards".

Take your Uncle Me'Shorn's advice: take this rule to heart. Just as stars cannot shine without the darkness, it is only in the darkest moments of your life that you can feel the light coming from you. Accepting, embracing, and embodying this light is up to you; make the right choice.

***

But just as skeletons provide a framework for our lives, other frameworks exist on a larger scale.

Frameworks can unite a diverse variety of concepts, ideologies, thought patterns, theories, and standards into large, singular bodies. These frameworks influence everything from the most transient narratives to the very fabric of reality as we perceive it.

I became conscious of this when I found myself in a setting utterly alien to me – one that alienated me even further from the world around me. The framework of my identity was shattered, and I saw beyond; everything I thought I was, was disproven. The beginning of MeShorn's is old, and my roots stretch back years back through time.

But the roots of this book, perhaps, are tied back to this event. This was when I truly realized that I am not America's black. It can be tied back to the events I witnessed in–

Louisville.

> *"I'm from Louisville, Kentucky, and **nobody** gets out of there... So it took [me] some time. The struggle made merealize I didn't really want to be **'normal'** anymore."*
>
> Bryson Tiller.

Before I went to Louisville, Kentucky, I didn't even know it existed; funny enough, I first heard the name when I was in West Germany, of all places. I had never heard of Louisville, but little did I know how much it would change who I fundamentally was.

It was indeed here that I truly grew to appreciate just how domesticated, indoctrinated, and subjected to an inferiority complex the people were. It was here that I made the awful discovery of what exactly it meant to be black in America.

***

Now, the history of Louisville, Kentucky, spans a bit over two whole centuries, but Uncle MeShorn will shorten it for you.

Back in the day, it was used as hunting grounds by natives; but with the coming of the Europeans, the Ohio River made it inevitable that a town would grow on the site. Sure enough, Louisville, Kentucky, soon became a thing in the 18th century. The very year the city was established in 1828, it also received some three-hundred-odd settlers.

Growing to be a major trade and industrial center, the city hit a speed bump in the mid-20th century. When it did pick itself back up in the late 20th century, Louisville decided on a new tactic; it adopted the framework of a 'culturally-focused' city.

In 2003, the city was transformed into the Louisville-Jefferson Metro area via a merger. Today, Louisville is the largest city in Kentucky and is the 29th largest city in the the country.

And then, there's...

The West End of Louisville, Kentucky.

Behind all this progress, Kentucky had once grown into one of the fifteen original Slave-states that had specialized in engineering American slavery throughout America. This was especially true for the urban community called the West End.

The West End emerged as a predominantly black-identifying neighborhood in the city of Louisville during the 1830s. Back then, the free blacks began buying property west of 9th Street, creating an infrastructural and racial divide that would lead to one of the most startling political realizations I would ever have.

When the city revitalized itself in the late 20th century, it did its best to try and hide the stains of slavery and segregation under claims of 'culture'. Liberal policies were enacted to rebrand racism as respect, segregation as the spirit of community, and the ghettos as diversity. And as the city continued to enact these neo-plantation concepts, America was happy to have her. Because America is always happy to have new echo chambers.

***

But of course, your Uncle Me'Shorn didn't know all this history back when I went to live there. I'd only arrived after retiring from the Army and marrying my wife, living for 24-plus years as a senior, non-commissioned officer.

Now, I had always been a man who ascribed to what it traditionally meant to be a man: breadwinner, provider, and protector. To my mind, that is what I was: a Man, not a black man.

But in Louisville, I could not escape the aforementioned color construct; I could not escape my own appearance. The Louisville community was stifling. It left me breathless, confused, and isolated, alienated in the place that should have soon become home to me. Yet in this place, every day, I felt like I was navigating and daily crossing over into the blackness of a sunken, fallen.

Louisville, you see, was a democrat's paradise – and hell for anyone who wasn't fanatically indoctrinated into that framework. As a traditional, relatively conservative person, I felt isolated and quarantined in 'enemy territory'. To speak bluntly, it felt like a perverse mixture of a racist plantation and an amusement park. One could even imagine a name for this bizarre haven: "The Wonderful of Liberal World of Victimization".

Every day, I would get up, kiss my wife, and immediately prepare myself like a military officer off to complete a dangerous mission. As you can imagine, it was hardly a welcoming atmosphere – the whole place was stuck in an echo chamber, constantly regurgitating the same things over and over.

What I saw in Louisville was beyond words. One of the few things I can even describe is the segregation – yes, the segregation! Beyond 9th Street for work, I would find myself in the medical, professional environment of the Operating Room. The majority of women and men here were of European demographics – an undeniable example of America's concept of 'white'. My principles, personality, and standards kept me afloat among them, and hell, I was getting paid a damn good income.

But then, after work, I found myself leaving this professional atmosphere and returning to the community deep inside the West End. A 'democratic' community full of unprincipled, morally decayed people who continued to identify themselves as the American Black.

The 'black minority' here had accepted second-class citizenship. It had adopted the very racist caricature put upon them and worsened it. To my horror and dismay, these people had grown to exemplify the racist, derogatory jokes hurled against us for years. They reminded me of the craze I had seen after the release of Roots. They had developed an entire subculture based around a 'white bogeyman,' blaming the republican party as being the only racist political party in America.

As I watched with a terrible sense of awe, I began to realize what it meant to become the American black.

***

But this was only the beginning of my realization, a realization that came to completion after an event called the Louisville Kentucky Derby.

Now this Kentucky derby, predictably taking place in the West End, was like nothing I'd ever witnessed – underneath a veneer of color and culture that I instantly saw through was a display of the most profound depravity. What I saw that day was so profoundly unnatural that I will not repeat it – and you know for a fact that Uncle Me'shorn hasn't pulled any punches so far. Even considering the terrible things in my past, my roots, that I have put to paper, there are some things that I must hold back.

All I will say is that it was the most profound shock – and it spurred me to the realization that no matter what, I could never fit into the absurd, depraved 'normalcy' of Louisville. We were alike only in the melanin in our skin – in creed, character, and faith, we were miles apart. That is how I realized that these were people who were lost in a framework utterly alien to me – and utterly destructive to the moral fiber of this country. And this is when I realized there was something else at play, something invisible and malevolent.

But looking back, it's interesting how I ended up in West End, of all places – interesting how I ended up surrounded by men and women celebrating their own enslaved natures. Whatever innocence I had left after the darkness of my past was lost that day – and once it was lost, I knew there was no way to turn a blind eye anymore.

There was no way to look away. I had to face the fact that these things were occurring throughout America. The country I had once served.

And so, I swore to myself that day not to repeat what I had seen. What happens in Vegas shall stay in Vegas – and what happens in Louisville shall stay thereat. There was no point repeating the event; the only real point, I knew, was to emerge from it like a warrior on a mission, like a wanderer in a desert, like a vagabond seeking his path. No matter the cost.

What your Uncle Me'Shorn witnessed there was enough to scare anyone. It certainly scared me.

And that is why I am not your black, America.

***

But like a man who has begun to see after a lifetime of blindness, I was terrified of my discovery. I couldn't understand, at first, the organized horror of what I had perceived – this absurd, horrific layering of frameworks. Skeletons, not on a personal level, but on a national and global scale. Carefully inflicted wounds to the heart and mind of America, frameworks designed to bind, blind, and deceive us.

It would take me some time to realize what I was looking at. It would take me time to realize that I was staring the enemies of this country right in the face.

What I had begun to see, like apparitions in the dark, were the mass frameworks holding this world together, strung between reality and ideology.

And what were these frameworks? Well, they're called–

Part II
Paradigms

Color Construct.

*"Scientifically, anthropologically, racism is a **construct** — a **social construct**."*

Toni Morrison.

Paradigms are a compound of concepts, beliefs, ideologies etc., that have merged into a singularity. Paradigms, by their very nature, unite on the basis of similarity – therefore, a paradigm is necessarily an over-simplification. Paradigms don't reflect the truth but rather reduce the complexity of truth into easily understandable, effortlessly consumable archetypes.

Due to how easy to believe paradigms are, their manufactured version of reality ends up seeming more real than the truth; it feels more visceral, immediate, and simple. Paradigms give you a ready-made world, a belief to inhabit, and an entire system to buy into.

But Uncle Me'Shorn, you ask. How do paradigms come into being?

Straightforward question with a simple answer

– they don't come into being! They're made, constructed, and molded; they are the work of human hands, the product of mortal minds. Even the most 'organically' formed paradigms are still the result of human belief.

Paradigms are not intrinsically bad – after all, a definite degree of order and structure is needed for society to function. However, the problem with paradigms is a problem of transparency. Now, what does that mean? While some paradigms are clear, open, and transparent about their constructed nature, others try to pass themselves off as normal, natural, and inherent. Therefore, this latter sort of paradigm is a case of 'false advertising'.

For example, even the economy is technically a construct – but it's an open construct. I don't think I'm wrong if I say that everyone and their mother knows that humans created the economy. It's no hidden fact that it's not 'natural'.

But the problem arises when a narrative proclaims that it is, in fact, a part of objective reality. Those fooled by the paradigm confuse it with the reality in front of their eyes to the point where they cease to see anything except the paradigm they ascribe to. Therefore, the 'painting' or image created by a paradigm can also be used to hide or obfuscate an obvious truth behind an elaborate lie that serves someone's agenda or purpose.

There are many paradigms at work in modern America – and far too many are inherently deceptive in nature. In such situations, it becomes increasingly vital to call these false descriptors of reality out and expose them for what they are: human constructs.

And one of the most prolific of these constructs, one of the primary reasons behind writing this book, is the color construct that is at work behind this country.

***

What is the color construct?

It is the division between black and white so deeply rooted within American culture. It is the division formed in Europe with the advent of colonialism, the divisive paradigm that has endured for centuries and continues to thrive in this country's alleyways and institutions even today. The color construct is the ghost that haunts our nation; it is the wall that denies entry or normalization, emphasizes opposition, eliminates compromise.

No visual representation of contrast is more striking than white and black, and whenever two opposites collide, the question of superiority arises. The objective of the contrasting narrative is to create conflict, even where there is none – because conflict leads to victors and losers.

Conflict is always a question of superiority, and superiority is always an exercise of power, be it through force, coercion, or even moral authority. To pit white and black against each other is to ensure that one side wins – and most of the time, this means that the 'black' loses.

America's Black is an object – to be a 'black man' is to be the shadow of a 'white man'. These are both archetypes, and oversimplifications, but effective nonetheless.

America is unable to think beyond these simplifications now. We cannot look beyond – we are stuck looking at skin and color.

The construct has engineered a lens through which we must see color, we must see race.

Ironically, even the very concepts of color and race are connected intrinsically to America. The history of this continent is the very birthplace of division; it is the very hub of scientifically standardized othering. Born from the initial enthusiasm around the secular sciences emerging in the Judeo-Christian world order, racism was the initial paradigm succeeded by the subtler color construct. This racial paradigm divided peoples and ethnicities into shorthand races for the 'ease' and 'convenience' of the average European.

With the advent of colonization, the N-word was suddenly applicable to all individuals who shared certain physical features or ethnicities; Indians of all religions suddenly became known as the 'Hindoo race'; meanwhile, much to their confusion, the many Native peoples in the Americas began to be called 'Injuns' by the Europeans.

This shorthand meant for rich Europeans too unbothered to talk to any of the locals was further bandied around by researchers. Suddenly, race had become a 'scientific fact'; journals and diagrams described racial differences and features with absurd details directly scrounged from cursory eyewitness accounts. The race construct was thus created by a bunch of wealthy, clueless men too disinterested to do any real research involving the people they were busy labeling.

Perhaps the most terrible effect this construct has had isn't even the loss of identity many cultures went through – it's that people began to relate to and accept these genuinely stupid labels. People from marginalized communities began to self-identify with their labels. Instead of seeing the shackles of race-terms and colored language that held them down, people began to use these very shackles as a makeshift identity.

What can a man say to that? God knows I understand feeling lost, but to cling to your chains and calling them medals of pride is hardly a healthy coping mechanism! Even if it provides temporary solace, it's just that – temporary. It's a delusion.

This hard-racism paradigm has, over the years, transformed into its own, 'softer' successor: the color construct. Instead of simply allowing a one-way categorization, the color construct is significantly more devious because it allows both 'sides' of the color spectrum to openly declare allegiance to the construct on equal terms. By rebelling against all that is 'white', we pledge to the 'black', and, therefore, indirectly continue to serve the same construct.

***

When I see people going mad for black pride, I ask them: What is black? What exactly does this word even represent?

They answer that it means African-American.

Then why do you keep saying black? I'll tell you why – an African American in this country is bound to the color construct by the invisible laws that control this nation.

People talking about African-American pride often recourse to Africa for their myth – they sell the myth of one Africa, a whole, unbroken past of 'blackness', some mythical heaven for the 'black race'. But no such thing exists: there is no black race. The entire concept is the result of an oversimplification made by colonizers that were too uninterested in learning the local customs of the African continent and the various peoples, ethnicities, and tribes that dwelled thereat.

The Zulu tribes of South Africa, for instance, don't have much in common with the Coptic (Al-Qibt) peoples of Egypt and Sudan; the Igbo tribes of the west similarly don't self-identify with the Maasai people of Kenya. To the American mind, they may all qualify as 'black', but that is only the paradigm talking; skin color doesn't enter into their identity, which is based more on their culture, history, and roots than anything.

Why would they recourse to race when they have their past?

Their roots run deeper than skin.

Skin is the final recourse for those with no past

– which is what 'black' Americans really are – American Descendants of Slaves. We are Americans by nationality, but not when it comes to rights or participation; we exist on the fringes of society. We languish in slums. Instead of dreaming of glorious pasts that adhere to the color-construct that constricts us, we must train our eye to look into the past to see the future. We must unlearn to relearn.

This is the only way to combat deceptive constructs – they must be systematically unlearned. The construct is lodged into the human mind like a tumor that slowly grows, consuming and subverting everything in its wake. It absorbs memories, filters experiences, subverts narratives, and censors anything against it. It is not enough to work from the outside; constructs can also manipulate you from within.

Constructs like the color construct inhabit two separate spaces – on the one hand, they exist in the real world as philosophies and agendas that define the scopes, objectives, and biases of various institutions and systems. On the other hand, there are also internalized constructs – which is to say that an individual who is exposed to a paradigm for long enough internalizes it entirely. The internalized construct does not need outside help to manipulate an individual; it's like a spy living inside your own brain, a ghost in the inner-matrix.

So, what does this mean?

It means that you can't learn the truth until the dominant construct has been dislodged. The color construct – and all others like it – must be unlearned. Nothing can grow on salted earth; first, you must cull the soil and fertilize it before you can grow anything in it.

It is hard work, but the bounty of the harvest is worth the effort.

***

Some of you might be asking right about now: But Uncle Me'Shorn, why does the color construct exist? What is its purpose?

Well, I'll tell you.

As I said, some deceptive constructs / paradigms attempt to create questions of power, superiority, and dominance. The creators of the color construct want to establish something that a fellow called Gramsci described as a hegemony.

What that means is that the color construct exists to create sides, thereby elevating one 'side' so much above the other that its dominance is unchallengeable.

The construct creates an illusion of equal power. It tells you, 'Of course you're black, but don't worry – you can campaign for black rights too'. But ultimately, by supporting 'black rights', you become Their Black; you become another part of the game, another cog in the machine. By struggling against the lure of 'white dominance', you actually accept their hegemony – their absolute dominance. As long as you play by the rules of their discourse, their narrative, their story, you will be their black.

You tell me: how could any power be more dominant than if they could create and control the very rebellion against themselves?

By trying to fight hegemony, people end up using the very narrative created by the hegemonic power: the very questions they know how to answer, the very arguments they know how to disarm. It's like waging war with weapons provided by the enemy and being surprised when the gun goes off in your face!

Go off the beaten path – find a better answer.

***

If I was a pessimist, I'd say that the color construct has ruined us.

It has instilled this helpless sense of inferiority that persists through the communities, pulls us down, and makes us believe we are worth exactly what they say we are. I've seen men ashamed of their ancestors, ashamed of where they came from, ashamed of how they look; I've seen people so deeply caught in the trap of the construct that they want to either act 'white' to fit into affluent society or act 'black' to fit in with other African-Americans. My own grandfather – rest his soul – married a woman simply so his children would be 'black enough' to fit in.

But God is good, and I'm not pessimistic enough for that sort of defeatist talk. Me'Shorn T. Daniels is a man of hope.

They tell me, do not hope. You'll get disappointed.

We're headed toward dystopia.

I say we already live in one – that's why we need to hope! Hopes, prayers, and knowledge are the only way forward.

This terrible sense of institutionalized, internalized inferiority must be defeated. The narrative must be unwoven and unlearned; the people must learn to see themselves as something other than what the construct tells them they are. They aren't 'black' or 'persons of color'; that's a term of abuse. That's what they used to call segregated schools – colored schools. I shouldn't need to say that to take pride in that is perverse.

We have lived with their labels for so long that many of us have become them. We have accepted our 'place' in a manufactured hierarchy that is passed off as natural; we have become part of an invisible caste system that lulls us with ironic slogans of freedom while imprisoning us in the consensual prison of color and race. We enter their educational institutions, and what would you know? They're still colored; rich schools produce the idea of 'white' and schools in the ghettos reinforce the 'black' identity we grow up with.

The first-glance-passed paradigm America projects – the FGP – is a color construct allowing the white immediate access, protection, and privilege. The same is true for the Jewish community and any and all immigrants who immediately received this equal status because of their ability to be First Glance Passed. However, they did not earn this passage, not being homegrown Americans. Since Bacon's Rebellion, the industrialization of the fifteen original seedling Slave States in the South, a class of the people who are now the American Descendants of Slaves (ADS) have been put aside on the back burner, while all who pass the FGP are given equitable status.

The original and 'made in America' demographic in this country is the folk who are the descendants of the firstborn generation American Slaves from Jamestown, Virginia, from August 20th, 1619, to 1865. These 21st-century American descendants of Slaves effectively carry over a 400-year tradition. As a color construct in America, whiteness and lightness have provided immediate access to Zionist immigrants; they have taken advantage of the nonverbal FGP paradigm. They have facilitated a culture of alienation, a culture whereby the color construct allows for eternal othering between white and black, light and dark.

The othering never seems to stop. It is seen in labels at war, and false identities in conflict. Sane spirits are put down by both sides, called upstarts by some and traitors by others.

You ask: Uncle Me'Shorn, how do we get through this? How do we leave the construct?

Simple answer?

Reject their labels. Reject their colors.

Become the self that is untainted by the paradigm; recognize that there is no inferiority, no superiority, no sides, no races – reject the fragmentation they have enacted on God's people.

Reject the construct.

Become yourself.

***

Myths, paradigms, and constructs.

It's a strange world to be living in, a harsh one. It's not as clear-cut as the dystopias in the movies; there are layers to this hell. But it's a hell we're all forced to endure, even though few have what it takes to fight it. If you've read this far, I believe you have what it takes.

Giving up is easy. What's hard is to stand tall when everyone else bows and scrapes before the established events. It's not easy to keep going in these bleak times, but those who keep God in their hearts will always find a way. No one expects you to be fearless – no one expects you to have no doubts, to have no moments of weakness. God knows we all have those – I certainly do.

The brave man isn't the guy who never felt fear in his life – he's the guy who felt afraid but continued on anyways. Forget being fearless, be steadfast instead; be like stone, the sea, the deep roots that stretch under this earth. Have the bravery to continue to be the truest you can be before yourself and God.

The enemy is at the gates. Their forces are made of construct upon construct, layers of deceptive paradigms; they will try to convince you of failure, just as they tried to convince me of the same.

They called me names for not adhering to the corrupt, delusional color construct that this country so loves.

They called me a madman. They called me a 'traitor'. They called me–

Uncle Tom.

> *"Write on my gravestone: 'Infidel, Traitor.', infidel to every church that **compromises** with wrong; traitor to every government that **oppresses** the people."*
>
> Wendell Phillips.

The man who rejects hate in a time of hatred is never loved by his people; he is never accepted, nor do the masses respect him as much as the fiery revolutionary, even if the latter leads them into certain doom. Many folk love to talk about peace, but when it comes to taking the first step towards it, they'd rather wave baseball bats.

This is a reality that wasn't immediately obvious to your Uncle Me'Shorn. I was a younger, more naïve version of myself once – I believed that most people could generally be made to see sense. I thought that if you were calm, collected, and reasonable enough, people would heed you.

Turns out, people would rather follow demagogues and false prophets instead of a reasonable man; people would rather deviate towards extremes rather than opt for any middle ground. America's Black, for instance, sees only color – and when you try to look beyond the construct, they give you labels and epithets, resorting to petty name-calling.

***

Prior to my promotion to sergeant, I was an

E-4 surgical tech. Thus most of the folk who would later serve under me began as my peers – we were, at this point in time, all on equal rank. So I knew them relatively well, and they knew me.

This rapport with my peers was possibly one of the considerations that led to my promotion to an E-5 sergeant. Suddenly, I was given the responsibility and charge over these men and women, and it was a responsibility I felt very keenly. Now at this point, I'll also mention that these soldiers were from many ethnicities and walks of life, of both genders as well; but one thing that has been a constant in my life is that I've never differentiated between God's people on the basis of 'race' or gender. Even before I consciously knew its name or face, I rejected the racial paradigm that festered within this country.

But there's a point to mentioning this part of my life – it's a good example of what I'm talking about here.

At some point, my superior – a certain E7, Sergeant First Class Wellington – charged me with a certain task. Now when you get assigned a task by your senior, what is your first concern? It's to look good! You want to leave a good impression on the man – you want the task done properly. And when you need something done properly, you pick folk based on two things: skill and efficiency.

Turns out it doesn't work that way in America.

It just so happened that the folk I picked for the task – all of whom were very capable individuals I had previously served with – were unhappy with the choice. Why? Because they were all 'black'; they had the color identity engraved in their minds to the point where color was the only thing they cared about. And so, their concern with the task wasn't about the task at all; it was about the self-victimizing paranoia the construct had instilled in them. They cursed me for choosing them over the 'white man' – they wanted me to make the 'whites' do the task, even though I very much found them more suited to the task.

Any task or job has key, practical considerations, and race isn't one of them. Why would I, of all people, judge a person based on the melanin in his or her skin? Should we put quotas on every little task, and try to please every demographic? What about efficiency or merit?

Should I have simply put a 'white' soldier onto the team just to appease them, even if it reduced the overall efficacy of the task at hand?

According to them, yes. According to America, yes.

And so, these folk started slandering me, telling all sorts of tales, giving me all sorts of names.

One of these names was 'Uncle Tom'.

***

Well, now, you ask, what does that mean? Who is Uncle Tom?

Uncle Tom is a generally a derogatory term that, in essence, translates to 'race traitor'. It's as stupid a term as they come, made on the prior assumption that the primary loyalty of a man should be to 'his race'. It is a color loyalty inculcated, groomed, and indoctrinated in the minds of America's black – and breaking the construct for them is easier said than done, as your Uncle Me'Shorn can attest.

Now, this 'Uncle Tom' title is based on the title character of several plays and a novel by Harriet Beecher Stowe called Uncle Tom's Cabin.

The book recounts the story and life of an enslaved person named Tom, who is beaten to death for refusing to betray the whereabouts of two other slaves. In the book, Uncle Tom is portrayed as a heroic character loyal to the slaves in hiding. He's shown to be a good man in bad times. But racist producers of stage adaptations later distorted the character into being intensely loyal to 'white' people.

Therefore, the character suddenly became known as an archetypical race traitor, even though it defeats the original point of the book!

The point was that Uncle Tom wasn't loyal to black or white; he was a slave loyal to his brethren. He was a man of God in godless times who suffered great pain for his people.

But the flagrant narrative of Uncle Tom-ism bandied around in modern African-American communities is a perversion. It is based on race constructs and ideas that have been put into our heads by the arch-racist of the past – it is the carnival retelling by old, racist men that have somehow created an Uncle Tom Construct in our heads.

Yes, Uncle Tom, too, is a construct. It is a constructed 'punishment' for not adhering to the color construct; it is the threat they use. It is the tool used to socially exile, ostracize, and ridicule those who don't play by their rules. Those who dare to look behind the curtain. Those who try to do the right thing at the wrong times. It is a phrase that flies in the face of the humanism that America is supposedly founded on – it rejects the sovereignty of man's viceroy-authority under God, using the color construct to divide between men as though we were breeds of animals.

Why should a man be loyal to his color? Why should we be categorized based on the melanin in our skin? Are we like children that cannot see past blues and greens? You would think there are nobler ideals, beliefs, and causes to pledge yourself to – but instead of ascribing to any belief that may unite us, we have been conditioned to only feel united in our differences. We have been conditioned to only feel comfort or a sense of belonging within our respective communities so that we can never present a united front. And any man who dares to look beyond is named a traitor.

It is a strangely extreme narrative, which is perhaps why it appeals to so many. The Uncle Tom construct is a part of a wider 'with us or against us' narrative – it is founded on a perceived shared, radicalized identity that does not allow for any dissent. This is the key part: it is a narrative that isn't content with convincing or indoctrinating – it utilizes the fear of being socially outcast as a (generally efficient) form of coercion. Remember, whenever a narrative is using power or threats to assert itself, it is always both coercive and deceptive – a well-intentioned discourse that is wholesome in its contents will never resort to the exercise of power.

The color construct reinforces itself through the carrot and stick approach. What's a carrot and stick approach? Well, suppose you have a donkey

– you want it to do exactly what you want. You have two ways of making it follow your instructions. You can either wave a carrot in front of its face and reward it when it obeys, or if it fails to be obedient, you can hit or threaten it with a stick. This is the basic principle of reward and punishment.

Similarly, the color construct utilizes carrots and sticks – it rewards people for sticking to the construct by giving them a feeling of belongingness, a feeling of being 'one of the group'. It gives you a readymade, easily accessible identity, a future, and a link to a past (be it real or manufactured), providing you with a general feeling of 'knowing your place' in the American hierarchy. If you don't abide, however, the construct utilizes the stick – which is the Uncle Tom construct, the race-traitor narrative, the color-loyalty paradigm.

***

Once upon a time, there was a little bump in history called the French Revolution. Don't worry, your Uncle Me'Shorn isn't about to give you a history lesson – but it illustrates the point well.

This revolution was against the King, and the folk rebelling were understandably upset with the French courts' greed, corruption, and unsavory lavishness. So they went ahead and created socio-political upheaval, took up arms, and chopped the fellow's head off.

But what happened next? The extreme nature of their freedom paradigm consumed them. They grew obsessed with absolute freedom; from the King, they moved on to killing his wife. From there, they started killing the rich. From there, they started killing anyone whose hands were 'too soft' to be poor. And finally, they started executing the moderates, anyone who told them they might be going too far.

Never trust a narrative or paradigm that persecutes the moderate-minded or reasonable folk who aren't swept up in incendiary fervor at the drop of a hat. Beliefs and convictions are good, but if you need to persecute folk for not being as fanatical as you, there's a problem. Whether it is by carrots or sticks, discouraging moderate discourse should always be a red flag – yet, it always seems to invite even more enthusiastic dissent.

The middle path is thus abandoned for an extreme. In fact, I've found that America and many of 'her black' hate the middle ground. The idea of being moderate is despicable to many because being moderate requires you to have a self-identity and self-assurance; unlike picking extremes, picking the reasonable option doesn't provide you with a readymade persona to fit into. They aren't interested unless there are costumes, face paints, or catchy little bits of rhetoric to scream out at passersby's.

These folk are the same that drag others into their respective extremes. They pull you down a spiral of uncertainty, then launch you forth onto that rollercoaster ride of radicalization. Suddenly, incremental progress isn't good enough no more; suddenly, you start using words like 'the blood of tyrants' and 'us or them'. You become convinced in the myth being forced down your throat to the point where you consume it willingly; soon, you develop a taste for the horrific discourse, and your appetite can only be whetted by indulging in it.

Others are relatively moderate internally but are forced to play along with extremist narratives out of the fear of Uncle Tom-ism; believe me, no one likes to be taunted by their brethren. Uncle Me'Shorn knows that better than anyone – but a man, a true man, must take a stand. We can't let ourselves be pulled into the throng of blind buffoons; we must maintain our inner selves and stand for what we believe in.

***

Speaking of taking a stand, it's important to be careful about the cause you choose to stand for; not all stands are worth taking.

I'm talking especially about the recent trend of race-based stands that have caught like wildfire through America. I'm talking about the resurgence of that extremist hate I saw in the wake of Roots.

I'm talking about the young people driven astray by errant, careless ideologies espousing division, harm, and violence against their fellow countrymen.

I'm talking about the phenomenon that is known as BLM – 'Black Lives Matter'.

What a name: Black lives? What black lives? Since when do experiences have color? I'm sure you'll agree that the Creator didn't design humans with pre-made 'black' and 'white' lives. Life is life, and our experiences are our experiences; life isn't a pair of sunglasses. It doesn't need color to set it apart.

Lives are inherently unique and diverse – but these differences come from how we live them, not on the basis of skin-identities, not unless you make it so. It's like what they call a self-fulfilling prophecy; if you keep seeing everything in terms of the color construct, the paradigm comes true for you. If you accept a 'black life', that's all you're about to get. You'll be stuck in the loop, stuck in living someone else's idea about who you are or who you should be. Soon enough, the man is consumed, and only the black remains. You are lost in the myth of someone else's making.

BLM is a paradigm that thrives on Uncle-Tom- ism. It thrives on race loyalty; the narrative's flagship arguments are founded on skin politics.

The BLM narrative is particularly dangerous and irresponsible because it targets the youth; it inculcates the belief in them that Black Lives Matter

therefore, they matter more than others. This is a dangerous understanding; it can – and has – created swathes of hate among the people based on nothing but color. It is a hate that spreads on the streets, in establishments, and even in schools

it is all-consuming.

The construct feeds on conflict. As long as people continue to buy into conflict narratives like BLM, they will continue to be enslaved by the shackles of race and color; they will continue to be used and discarded by ideologies.

***

Uncle Tom is a fallacy; he is a catch-all for every dissident, every moderate, and anyone who speaks up with even a hint of logic or reasoning.

So no, I am not 'Uncle Tom'. I am not a traitor, for I never pledged allegiance to your definition of me; I never identified as your black. I am not your black, America – I have never been your black. I am my own man, and my loyalty is my own, my causes are my own, and my stands are my own. I reject your racialism. I reject your colorism. I reject your extremism.

I am a man among men, a human amidst humans. My law is the law of God, and my people are the reasonable ones, regardless of the pigmentation of their skin. I am not a traitor, for I am loyal to my beliefs, and I stand by my choices, my faith, my convictions; I stand by my proclamation that we are more than race, more than melanin, more than the identities you have sorted us in.

Keep your labels, for I reject them. Keep your sticks, for I am unafraid. Keep your carrots, for I am satisfied. Keep your myth, for I doubt–

Your 'Great' America.

> *"It's the movies that have really been running things in America ever since they were invented. They show you **what** to do, **how** to do it, **when** to do it, how to **feel** about it, and how to **look** how you feel about it."*
>
> Andy Warhol.

As I said prior, our world is made of myths and paradigms – and one of the most prominent paradigms in this country is this country itself. The narrative of a 'Great' or otherwise whole America has been constructed through a shared mythology that we consume through television, books, the internet, and general media.

This collection of media, myths, narratives, and stories, have created a situation where the truth of America has been obfuscated behind a shiny veneer. A marble façade hides the true problems behind America; it is a mask created by smiling political figures and the political-entertainment complex to blind the average American to the dystopia he or she is living in.

This is 'Great America' – the myth of what America

Says It Is.

***

I believe in America. I do.

But I believe in the potential of America. I believe in the principles behind America. I'm a patriot; I believe in the earnest truth of the ideology itself behind this country, not in the way it has been enacted thus far.

Many folks think that patriotism just means standing by your country no matter what it does or just waving a flag without putting any deeper level of thought into the condition of the state. But just as the state makes the man, the man makes the state, and if the American people continue to be servile, toothless, and uncritical, what can we expect of America? Let Uncle Me'Shorn tell you that without people to question the status quo, the status quo becomes a chokehold. The status quo, if left attended, leads to tradition, which leads to ritual, which leads to the paradigm of utterly deluded self-worship.

This is what the Great America paradigm is: it is shameless self-glorification of the status quo, the way things are. It is the belief that the America we currently inhabit is without fault or flaw and is some sort of perverse deity. In essence, it is the blindness of the people to the fact that their nation is slowly turning from a state to a cult, a cult where the leaders can brainwash them into believing all is sunshine and rainbows, even as the dark shadow of poverty, corruption, and debauchery swells in the forgotten hoods and ghettos of this country.

***

I doubt it's news to anyone that the media is very good at creating illusions.

That's what any semi-decent movie director does: he shoots the shot in a way as to convince the viewer that the scene he/she is looking at is, in fact, real. All movies are a product of movie magic, the process of creating the illusion of reality using your available resources.

One of the greatest illusions pulled off by modern media is convincing viewers of the success of this nation. It has created an illusion of normalcy, an impression of a righteous nation that has struggled through adversity to achieve a utopian era of eternal peace. The siren song of freedom is sung through movies – it is the attempt to convince the viewer of how free, equal, and borderline utopian this country is.

Everything from the color-grading of the films to the coloration of the casts to meet diversity quotas, creates the impression of 'the land of the free' that this country wishes it was. Bright, vibrant colors, scenes of industrious work, a 'racially diverse' cast, utter, ahistorical equality, and the normalization of all sorts of perversely sexual stances create the myth of an America that is whole and comfortable with itself. Meanwhile, on the streets, electoral slogans shout the names of saviors, appealing to various groups and demographics for a vote; advertisements specifically designed for 'black' people pander to bright, ethnic visuals to show how multicultural this country is.

But sadly, it's not. This shiny layer of greatness is an aggressive paradigm trying to subvert any criticism of America.

"How can we be racist?" say the Racists. "We always cast black and colored people in our movies!"

America's current supposed greatness is a shield to protect it from the critically minded. It is a sham designed to misdirect those who might otherwise wake to the oppressive constructs of this city.

Great America is a Matrix, and most of us can't wake up from it.

***

Some of you might ask, Now, what's a Matrix?

It's a complex answer, so let's approach it with the most popular usage of the term: the 1999 blockbuster science fiction movie The Matrix, which was instrumental in many ways in actually expressing the reality we inhabit – or think we inhabit.

The movie follows its protagonist through a dystopian world where humans are forced to live a simulated life by their oppressors. Living through their generated reality, people lose any concept of reality beyond their own – the mundane comfort of their squalid existence keeps them immune to anything that can break the illusion. After having part of the truth revealed to him, the protagonist is given a choice between forgetting what he has seen via a blue pill or having the entire truth laid bare before him via a red pill. Of course, the protagonist chooses the red pill.

However, most Americans do not. Most Americans follow authority figures and 'opinion leaders' with complete faith – figures propagating the toxic paradigms that entrap the people are common in this country. We are stuck in a simulation created out of constructs, a simulation that reassures us about what is normal and what is not, what is acceptable and what is not, and what is real and what is not.

Likewise, the American Matrix is a complex interconnection of politics, narratives, constructs, entertainment, and media. This Matrix is a collection of the experiences of the American people, the engineered experiences designed to create a group of people who are so thoroughly ensnared and enamored with the narrative that they cannot escape it; they cannot even consider escape because they love the matrix around them. The information network that constantly controls their inputs and measures their outputs likewise forms and informs their tastes and desires.

The American Matrix is run by the powerful, the figures that decide how deceptive constructs work and interact in America.

The matrix is in our norms, our clothing, and the music that is popularized. The matrix is like an all-permeating force – it is the network of strings that decides how this puppet-show around us works! The 'Great American Matrix' is thus a paradigm that consists of many other deceptive constructs – and the dangerous thing is that people love the idea of a mythical 'Great America'.

People ignore the red pill because it would open their eyes and demand an exit from the paradigm. And as I will discuss later, when you leave the paradigm... there is no going back.

But people always want a return. What most people want above all else is a past, memories, someplace to escape back into. It is a human instinct to want a past, to have roots, something anchoring you to history and your ancestors – yet, in many ways, this country has made this desire dysfunctional. It has created a construct that has replaced our desire for a personal past with a desire for a total, utopian past. Like Adam dreaming of heaven, we grow eternally more enamored of a mythical place in the past we have 'fallen' from.

And thus, many of us have grown to idealize the total past itself, seeing in it something that is missing from the modern world. We even use it as a coping mechanism! How's that? Well, we escape into the fantasy of the past to escape the horrors of today and the uncertainty of tomorrow. When the world seems like a big, scary place, instead of putting our big-boy pants on and taking the red pill as we should, we lapse into melancholic, wistful longing for a past world. Instead of standing up for what we believe in, instead of standing our ground, we opt for the easier way out.

In particular, to simply survive the horror of the upside-down America we live in, we escape into the 'Great America' delusion. We grow enamored with stories and posters, a veneer of greatness. But if there ever was some sort of mythical period of greatness in America, when was it?

Was it when folk came here and fought and killed each other for land? Was it when they brought African slaves to this continent to work the plantations? Or was it when wealthy European aristocrats could sup and dine on the privilege won from institutionalized slavery? Was it when people struggled in this country for the very right to live and breathe, humiliated for the color of their very skin?

To those who promise to make this country great again: When was America ever great?

***

But 'Great America' is more than just a false past – it is also a false present.

Certain figures have tried to brush away the issues plaguing this country by constantly trying to prove how great America currently is. These figures react with the hubris of an emperor being told that he might be wrong; they insist on the great situation of this country even when all evidence points to the contrary.

One of the prime examples of a figure exemplifying the Great America Matrix is one that 'America's black' loves: Barrack Obama, the first 'black' president of the United States of America.

Obama champions this paradigm; he champions the idea of an all-encompassing 'Great America' that stands above 'White' America, 'Black' America, 'Hispanic'

America etc.

Thus, Obama's America is an inherently colored, radicalized America; it is the color construct taken to its limits, normalized to the point of perverse pride. People love Obama because they believe he 'creates spaces' for all colors – but the truth is that his 'creation of spaces' is the act of creating differences, normalizing the fragmentation of the American people. He was not content with being a president, of course not. He needed to be the black president so that he could claim to represent an entire demographic while simultaneously increasing their association with the color construct.

Let Uncle Me'Shorn ask you: How do you create an unbreakable chain?

Simple. Create a chain no one wants to break.

That is what men like Barrack Obama have tried to accomplish; they have attempted to create a desirable collar, a golden prison that the prisoner loves. And in large part, it is not a failure

yet it's not a full success either, not as long as people continue to ask questions and look with a critical eye.

For instance: ask, who is Barrack Obama?

Why does he speak for an entire American demographic when he's got basically nothing in common with them?

Why does a man like Obama get so much respect

from people who never benefited from him in any shape, way, or form?

These questions, they are vital. Asking them is vital. Finding answers is vital.

***

I know the blue pill is comforting.

Trust me, I know how appealing the thought is to brush everything you see under the rug, refusing to look up at the giant meteor bearing down on you. Refusing to notice that something is horribly wrong. Ignorance is indeed bliss. It is the happiest state of being, but it's also not real.

You can have the best dream in the world and still wake up hungry and alone. Likewise, you can be seemingly completely happy and content using the paradigm of America's false greatness, but it is ephemeral joy. It's a cloud, a puff of smoke, a thin gauze to hold things together until they fall apart. And that's the truth; things are falling apart.

Things are out of joint. Nothing is as it should be; everything once considered obvious, logical, or even sacred is slowly subverted by the constructs we live among, even as we continue to idealize false images and false idols.

"There is nothing wrong in America," they chant, even as this country hurtles into an abyss. 'They' are those people who still believe, those who still have faith in the construct. Many will never admit they were wrong; many will never admit that the world they believe in so earnestly is false.

America will never admit her flaws to them, and thus, many will never see them. It is up to us, each of us, to look beyond on our own. We must scrape together the truth ourselves; we must not remain as America's gullible 'blacks', 'whites', or 'browns'.

***

So America neither is nor was great – but it still can be.

Forget thinking about how great America once was. Forget thinking that you live in the greatest America that ever was. Only focus on tomorrow, on the future – a subject I will explain later in detail, but all you need for now is to tell yourself this:

Make America greater than it's ever been.

This is the only way America can ever realize the myth that it could never live up to. It must stop trying to justify itself or return to some non-existent past. America must hold itself accountable to a promise of true improvement. True change.

Only then can this country take its first toddler step toward greatness.

As for individuals, we must abandon deceptive paradigms and instead move towards paradigms of our own making, or at least a construct that is in our–

Control.

*"You have power over your **mind** - not outside events. Realize this, and you will find **strength**."*

Marcus Aurelius.

What defines a man? What makes us different from beasts? What is the surest, most obvious indicator of our sapience, something upon which all of human civilization rests on?

That's right – self-control. The ability to restrain yourself. The ability to hold back the roaring tide of emotions, desires, fears, traumas, and all the other facets of the mess lurking in our subconscious. We can only function in society because we hold back and keep ourselves in check. A man must know how to control himself – if we can't control ourselves, we can't hope to have any control over what happens in our lives.

As we saw, deceptive constructs prey on this sort of helplessness – they pull the helpless and powerless into their orbit, indoctrinating them into the extant paradigms. The vast majority of American paradigms only function because the American people have been taught to depend on them – our society lacks any moderation, any self-control. We indulge in luxury and excess; in fact, we glorify it. We desire more, forever more – we need the newest objects, the richest food, and the most advanced technology.

America has no self-control.

This is why we must create our own control; we must hold ourselves true and strong to who we really are. The American paradigm can only be subverted by the act of creating a personal paradigm, a shell to inhabit, a protective persona that the outside construct cannot influence. The important part is to deny America's construct and the destiny this country has been manifesting for centuries; as individuals, we must each take the reigns of a new destiny, a new self-future controlled by ourselves.

***

For an example of self-control in your Uncle Me'Shorn's life, let's go back to an incident that happened many years ago – on and around September 11, 2001.

9/11 is very significant in my life.

Right after leaving the courtroom in E-Town, I was witness to the second plane as it headed towards the Twin Towers in New York. I was in the army reserves, and we were on all alert; then, I got a phone call. We were all requested to assemble and make all the arrangements. After calling home to my wife, I got back to work.

I was not at all prepared for any of this. I didn't know what was in store for me, yet I made contact with my Unit and got involved. As an E-7 surgical technologist in our 5010th Hospital Unit, I was asked to be a part of the security to protect the people in our community. Thus, I became the leading security person for our hospital unit. From that time, we were all working in shifts around the clock; many people, including me, were working overtime. So I ended up working at the hospital as well as collaborating with my Unit.

One Saturday evening, I decided that I'd worked non-stop for a long time – it was time for me to go home. Assigning one of my subordinates to be in charge, I left for home.

Two hours later, I received a phone call from the subordinate sergeant. He told me that Captain Jones was inquiring about my whereabouts and that she wanted me to take care of the unfinished work. I told the subordinate sergeant I'd already taken care of that work. So hung up the phone, but soon, I received yet another phone call.

Apparently, Captain Jones wanted me to come back to the Unit.

The next morning, around 3:45 am, Captain Jones and I reached the Unit simultaneously. We met at the parking lot, and we discussed my task, and I assured her that everything was in control. Yet, she told me to redo the work.

Now, I knew that her orders were baseless. She clearly hadn't even seen the work I had done! So when she ignored my efforts and insisted I redo the task, I turned to her and refused.

Notice: I did not allow her to cow me, but I did not act in an emotional, extreme manner. I remained calm under pressure, willing to hear her out but unwilling to go against what I stood for.

Taken aback by my refusal, she looked at me and said, "I am giving you direct order, Sergeant Me'Shorn Daniels, to carry on this specific orders that I require you to do."

Again, I refused.

"No, Ma'am. I am not doing it. You are disrespecting me and not looking at what I did already. And I am not going to do the same thing over again."

She told me flatly that since I had disobeyed her, she would take away the charge of the responsibility of security from me. But in some ways, I was ready for this, because I knew: actions have consequences. I had made my choice and was willing to follow through with the results.

And so, I stayed true to my word, acquiesced to her decision... and then left.

When I reached home, I got a phone call saying that Captain Jones had reported me for being a failure in my job, and she was filing charges against me for abrogating Article 15. So for about six months, I was under prosecution for not fulfilling my duty.

My confrontation with Captain Jones had crippling consequences. At the peak of my career, I was suddenly brought up on unfair charges that had nothing to do with my job. In other words, my accomplishments surrounding the E-7 surgical technologist became useless as I suffered these baseless charges. If you understand how the military works, you will surely understand my pain

because, in the military, there is no room for arguments. What your senior authority and, in my case, the company commander would say is pretty much binding. There wasn't any questioning, rebuttal, or cross-examination.

There was very little hope ahead for me, but I stayed resolute. Then I received a phone call from Command Sergeant Major Jefferson inquiring about what has happened with me. I explained everything in detail, and he assured me that he would look into this matter. Well, I didn't hear a word from the Command Sergeant Major for six months.

My hearing for Article 15 was brought up for the Uniform Code of Military Justice (UCMJ), and I was summoned to the stand. The company commander, Colonel Furry, was my commander. And asked me to report to them, and I reported:

"This is Sergeant First Class Me'Shorn T. Daniels, sir, reporting to you as you requested."

The commander asked me, "Sergeant, for what reasons are you standing before me?"

"Sir," I began. "I am standing before you because I been charged on disobeying a lawful order of the superior senior officer appointed over me, Sir!"

And the Colonel told me to sit my ass down.

I obeyed. Then he said to me:

"Sergeant Daniels, your character and your leadership have certainly preceded you. After a thorough investigation, we have discovered that Captain Jones only had ten service years to your twenty years. Not only does she lack time of service, but she is also inexperienced when it comes to leading Senior Noncommissioned officers. We have also found that the Captain has had multiple issues in her command."

As I watched in surprise, it became quickly apparent that they agreed that it was the Captain's failure to understand her leadership.

"The fact that you were an E-7 surgical technologist, and yet, were operating outside your capacity as a security officer in the wake of the 9/11 incident has also been considered," he continued. "Thus, we charge her and will verbally reprimand you. The Captain will receive a reprimand letter for disrespecting the historical contributions senior noncommissioned officers provide in the Armed Forces and under her command. So, Sergeant Daniels, you are dismissed, Article 15 has been dropped, and you can lead once more."

The commander's final verdict was a shock.

Later, I found myself on the phone with the Command Sergeant Major. He told me that multiple senior people had come to battle on my behalf, giving testimonies in my favor and clearly affirming my strength of character. Turns out that what had won me the case was the credibility that the Captain didn't have.

My conduct had created a credibility attached to the name of Me'Shorn T. Daniels that went beyond simple support. This was an example of what self-control in your everyday life can accomplish.

***

But Uncle Me'Shorn, you say, How do we achieve that sort of control?

I want you to imagine that you are a sword.

Now, why a sword? Because a sword's value, its intrinsic purpose and very usability depends on its sharpness, its ability to withstand impact, its ability to bend without breaking, and its ability to retain its edge.

Therefore, there are four key, defining elements of a sword that make it ready for battle: hardness, strength, flexibility, and balance. These are elements that you must inculcate within yourself – if you are to be a sword, that is to say a being with an internal, intrinsic purpose, you must keep these elements in mind. You must be tough yet flexible, strong yet balanced; therefore, you cannot push yourself to any extreme. Extremes are inherently unbalanced – they make you rigid and easy to influence.

Therefore, the first thing the individual needs to have self-control is to have a sense of self separate from ideology. The individual must not identify with any extreme or with any ideology at all to the point of being extreme himself; the individual must remember that the sword remains in balance. To have control means to begin from a place of neutrality.

This is, again, something missing in America.

This country does not believe in neutrality – it does not believe in finding a center, or an anchor, or anything that isn't a highly emotional, highly irrational ideological construct that powers itself from hate, trauma, fear, and insecurity. This mess of emotions and subconscious ramblings is thus built into this country's very fabric; everything that America claims to stand for is tainted by the darkness of its own uncontrolled urges.

When I say I am not America's black, I reject the paradigm and embrace the personhood. I reject the destructive and irrational discourse embedded into every institution, social construct, and public narrative spewed by the dominant forces of America. By denying America's black, I deny the entire contrast between white and black

I deny both extremes, for they have no basis in reality.

Thus, by denying the extremes, I am freed.
***

America is proud of her freedom: but this country's freedom narrative is flawed.

Freedom does not mean anarchy. Freedom does not mean complete abandon. Freedom does not mean utter debauchery and hedonism. What freedom means is responsibility –a key concept that must be understood. A man is responsible for his actions because all actions have consequences. Freedom doesn't mean that our actions cannot have unintended, unalterable, or otherwise unwanted results.

Freedom must be exercised with responsibility and control. When I rejected the Captain's demands in the aftermath of 9/11, it was not just to exercise my freedom. No, I had already completed my responsibilities – and even my rejection demonstrated self-control in its restraint. I refused the point that was actively against my decision and allowed the aftermath to play out – because I knew there is always a consequence.

You can never escape consequences, but you

can decide whether the consequences are worth it.

Every defeat, every heartbreak, every loss contains its own seed, its own lesson on how to improve your performance the next time.

MALCOLM X

He who can control himself can control the world outside him. As a fellow named Thucydides once said, self-control leads to self-reliance, and that leads to courage. As I said, the man who can control himself is the sharpest and strongest of swords because he has tempered himself in the forge of his own consciousness. Thus, the outside paradigm becomes unable to affect the person who can control themselves – it cannot undermine the self-paradigm of control.

Now that we have listed how to identify and push back against the deceptive forces of the constructs employed by this country, it is time to build our own wider paradigms – simple and true, without lies, trickery, or deception. To create a pure paradigm, we must return to the roots – not of an individual or ethnicity, but of mankind itself.

And if a man is to create something, all he needs are–

T.O.O.L.S. and W.O.R.K.

"The fall of humanity was the fall from the actual to thesymbolic."

Tony Vigorito.

Now, you might be thinking, what do these two phrases mean?

I could tell you upfront, but that would rob you of something, and that something is understanding. You could go into any school class and start telling children the meaning of complex terminologies from quantum physics, but they aren't going to understand it! Understanding any idea, any new concept, must come from building a progressive understanding of the subject. So instead of simply giving you definitions from the get-go, if you bear with me, I'll help you understand what they mean.

These concepts are also paradigms, but they are paradigms that go beyond human society – they enter into the realm of the human condition. Humanity is bound by these ideas and rules even if we do not want to be. These paradigms come not from man but from the universe – in essence, from God's creation. These are the paradigms that define the human and human experience. They also allow us to find meaning and purpose in our lives, because through these paradigms, the truly great men of this world succeed.

***

First, let us try to understand T.O.O.L.S.

Let's look at an example touching on two aspects that undeniably define the human experience, whether we realize it or not: history and faith. In that vein, let us look into the history of Christianity.

Before there was Christ, there was the figure of John the Baptist. Now, John the Baptist was meant to usher in Christ. He was meant to prepare the people for Christ's coming and also commit to the

faith himself. But although he laid the groundwork for Christ's arrival, he himself could not enter the complete fold of faith. Why? Because there were obstacles in his path. There was an element of limitation, an element of lack. This sense of limitation should be familiar to us all – we are all limited by our past, the narratives we ascribe to, the upbringing we have, the economic or social class we belong to, etc.

This very familiar limitation is what stopped John the Baptist from becoming a true member of the fold because he could not transcend his limit. He could not move beyond what was given unto him – he could not puncture the dome of his self.

Now take a closer look – what do these limitations remind you of?

Paradigms – the sort that hold us, bind us, and create a myriad of obstacles in our path. Deceptive paradigms that promise the world and deliver a needle, promise an easy solution and deliver a lifetime of alienation, rage, and anxiety. These paradigms are limitations – they are constructs that have been made to limit and contain the humanist spirit that this country claims to be founded on. The limitations are our shackles, our gags, and our iron cages. The fall of mankind was from heaven to reality and then from reality to symbolic constructs that have obscured every part of us. The original spirit of mankind has been lost in this construct.

So we must free it: but how do you break a construct?

With the right T.O.O.L.S.

T.O.O.L.S is an acronym symbolizing "To Overcome Obvious Limitations Spiritually". Since we now inhabit a world where meaning is constantly hidden behind paradigms, constructs, and symbols, we must use these things to defeat the overall matrix, the arch-construct we inhabit. As you can see, the symbolic importance of

T.O.O.L.S is that it offers a way to overcome the

limitations and constructs that limit us. It is the way for mankind to go beyond the limits placed upon them in this world.

How? It's in the name: through spirituality.

The limitations that bind us are mundane things. They feed on the anxiety they themselves cause, feed on our need for identity, for a shared connection, for anything to defeat the poverty, the alienation, the helplessness. When people lack any place in the world, they will cling to even the most absurd concepts, such as white and black. People will cling to colors as surely as a child to a rainbow because it gives them the illusion of belonging to something, coming from something, and being a part of something.

But ultimately, what is color? It is a delusion. All color is intrinsically subjective. Scientifically speaking, color is simply how humans experience various wavelengths of light. But we are so divorced from our true, essential natures that people will fight and die over what is, essentially, a subjective experience. It is a question without an answer, a war with no objective. No one can be right in an argument of 'who is better', when the very foundations of the argument are fictitious.

Yet the lighter you are in America, the more privilege you receive. This is the construct at work.

The delusions that dwell in reality stop us from

seeing it. If we want to acquaint ourselves to the real, true essence of ourselves, we must take the long way home.

What does that mean?

It means we must reach the Actual through the Spiritual.

Spirituality, which is faith or belief, has been around for as long as humankind has been around. It has always been mankind's tether, our lifeline to where we truly came from – our cosmic point of origin. That is our true, honest self, and it can only be reached by the spiritual.

However, spirituality is not only useful for beating the color/identity construct. It is a strong framework that allows one to weather the tarnished wasteland of everyday life. It has allowed your Uncle Me'Shorn to stay strong in the face of pain, adversity, and more challenges than I can count. It has allowed many to keep going when normal people would have given up. To face life with a spiritual outlook is the best way to look at and past the paradigms that limit us. It allows us to break our shackles, to overcome the constructs put in place to be obstacles for us.

John the Baptist couldn't enter the fold of faith entirely because he didn't have the T.O.O.L.S. He couldn't overcome the limitations of his time – even though he had the spiritual element, he could not successfully usher in Christ like he was supposed to.

Because though he had the spiritual element, he lacked the knowledge that the limitations of his times had to be overcome.

The Lord has given you all you need. He has given you the T.O.O.L.S you need to break the man-made matrix.

***

Who provides for the sparrow?

The Lord. It is He who ensures that the innocent little sparrow receives its fair share, that it doesn't go hungry. The nourishment it shall receive is preordained, which means that it is fated.

The sparrow is innocent. It exists in a realm of blessedness, blissful unknown, and a state of unstated euphoria. This is a state that finds a parallel in the religion-historical past of mankind; thus was the state of Adam and Eve, before they fell from Eden. In the Edenic myth, as told in the Bible, the original space Adam and Eve inhabited was the Garden, but after losing their innocence, they fell from grace. But was their greatest curse simply that they couldn't walk around in heaven's grass anymore?

No. It was a twofold punishment.

For one, they received awareness. They received the terrifying knowledge of their own bodies, their sexuality, and their physicality.

Suddenly, unlike any creature, beast, or animal, they felt shame – they felt inadequate, shameful, and dirty. The dirt in their lines became apparent to them, and it scared them. In short: their innocence was lost. And because their innocence was lost, they lost the state of euphoric bliss they once had. They lost the state of being like the sparrow the Lord provides for.

And what did that mean?

That meant that suddenly, the Lord wasn't providing for them anymore. No, now they had to provide for themselves.

They had to W.O.R.K.

***

Let your Uncle Me'Shorn tell you a story. I had never been brought up strongly

Christian, religious, or even particularly spiritual. I was told, however, to be religious; the problem was that I didn't feel it in my heart. So when I was told to simply repeat the verses, I refused. I have never been a dishonest man; I have always done my best to be direct, true, and honest at all times. But if I had recited the verses at that instance, I would have been a liar. I would have been dishonest to myself.

Yet after my first divorce, I remember driving home one night, almost alone on the road in my car, when suddenly I felt the urge to utter a phrase from the Bible. So at that moment, for the first time in my life, I uttered the syllables of Genesis from my mouth. I remember being overcome, overcome by a strong and sudden passion, a sudden emotion – coming to a halt, I felt as though the Lord himself was talking through me as I uttered the following phrase, "Me'Shorn, you have to work."

That's when I realized how true the phrase was. I realized how important work was in our lives – how humans must struggle and work to put a bite of food on the table. How we must fight for peace constantly. How we must constantly work to make things work so we can do the work we want.

This is where I derived the acronym W.O.R.K. from. As it is, it stands for Wisdom, Opportunities, Respect & Responsibility and Knowledge.

W.O.R.K is what we must do, what we must increase. Our T.O.O.L.S are what we use, but the W.O.R.K is what must be done. Each of these allows us to gain an insight that the Lord would have otherwise provided for; in a sense, W.O.R.K allows us to experience the fruit of our labors, the fruit the swallow receives for free.

Let's look at the elements of W.O.R.K, starting with Wisdom.

What is Wisdom? It is the ability to make the right decision. It does not involve knowing information or solving a problem. Rather, it is the ability to have the insight needed to look into the heart of the matter and make the right decision at the right time. Thus, it is a vital attribute that must be learned.

What about Opportunities? Opportunities are what are either made or discovered. These opportunities are like little windows toward success, profit, or simply doing something good. Opportunities, thus, must always be sought out.

What about Respect and Responsibility? A man must realize that he must respect others and respect the world in general. We don't live in a bubble; each man among us is a part of a society we all contribute to, effect, or are affected by. Thus we all have a responsibility to all those around us, especially our families and loved ones. Many turn their backs on the responsibility of their children and place them in the hands of others; more responsibility must be taken. By increasing the respect we have for others and the responsibility we feel in relation to them, we enrich our collective lives.

And what about Knowledge? This was originally almost a punishment for Adam and Eve, but it is also our path to salvation. There is no turning back; as I will explain later, humans cannot return to a prior state. Within our earthly lives, there is no return to paradise; there is no return to innocence; there is no return to bliss. But what we can do is keep moving forward. We must take what the Lord gave unto us – the seed of knowledge – and expand it. Learn more. See more. Unlearn the construct and Relearn the true knowledge that is very much our birthright as the descendants of Adam and Eve.

***

America must take up her T.O.O.L.S. Her people must increase their W.O.R.K.

This country has forgotten its spiritual lifeline; it has forgotten the true humanist ideals brought into this country at its inception. Although America never lived up to those ideals, they have remained here, simmering under this surface; they have remained, clawing at the earth to be realized.

Instead of trying to go back to reclaim a mythical origin by returning to a period of less knowledge and less W.O.R.K, America must move forward. Mankind must move forward. The construct must be subverted, and the limitations that bind us must be broken.

We must look ahead. We must move forward. And above all, we must keep our–

Part III
Beliefs

Epiphany.

"Epiphanies awaken the soul."

Adrienne Posey.

As you live your life, you come to realize many things. In fact, as far as your Uncle Me'Shorn is concerned, my life has very much been a collection of realizations. The more profound of these are what I refer to as epiphanies – ideas or realizations that completely blew me away and made me see the world in a whole new light.

Epiphanies can be painful or exultant, inspirational or destructive. They can be harbingers of positive change or even lead to an abyss. But ultimately, I believe that whatever the epiphany may be, arguably the most important part of it is how you react to it. An event certainly has an effect on you, but depending on how you choose to live with said effect, it can lead you in many, many different directions. I'm fortunate in many ways – God never overburdened me, and always gave me a way out of whatever storm I found myself in.

But insight is always destructive to some extent. Something must always shatter, be it your world-view, your paradigms, or your ego.

Something always shatters, but the shattering is necessary – someone who never breaks is never remade, and he who is never remade remains brittle. An epiphany forces you to reconsider your life, your views, and the whole world around you. In short, it forces you to unlearn that which you once 'knew' to be true.

And once you unlearn, only then can you

relearn.

****

One of the most important epiphanies I've ever had is a realization that occurred to me when I looked back to my own life. Usually, we take ourselves for granted; we're so utterly used to our pasts and identities that we do not see the subtle intricacies that act as clues for the astute mind. We only see what we expect to see.

Thus, by becoming lost in probabilities, we blind ourselves to the realities.

Yet your Uncle Me'Shorn, on one fine day, realized something. You see, I thought back to the day I was born: January 6, 1961. That's when I realized that there was something special about this day – it was Three Kings Day or the Feast of Epiphany, a day with spiritual, historical, and symbolic importance that is celebrated in Christianity.

I hear you ask, What does this day represent, Uncle Me'Shorn?

Let me tell you. This day represents the historical visit of the Three Kings/Magi to the cradle of the child Christ, who came to pledge fealty to Jesus. They gave unto Him gifts and affirmed his nature as both man and divine. But why did they leave their homelands in the East and come forth to find Christ? Because they felt the pull of truth. They felt their destiny calling unto them; they felt caught up in the desire put into them by the Lord's design.

And when they left their homes, the journey had to be made.

They could not go back. They could not return.

And so, Epiphany Day was my epiphany as well

the fact I was born on this very day made me realize that like the Three Kings, I was born to be a seeker, a wanderer going forth to find the Truth. I was a man who had left the familiar world of probabilities and familiarities; I had ventured into the desert of reality and found that metaphysical Truth was my purpose. I could not return; there was no going back. And so America, when you call me your names, when you call me mad, when you call me irrational, know that I cannot return to the sheepish, sleeping life you live. I have seen glimpses of reality, and he who has seen beyond the paradigms and the falsehoods can never return.

Innocence can be lost but never regained. In hindsight, that peaceful sensation of ignorance was never my home because the moment I left the cradle, I was met by the cold, harsh truths that crashed underneath the golden face of America.

My innocence was lost a long time ago; what is left is a man seeking the Truth, whatever it takes.

And this, America, is why I hold so true to my beliefs. Because, unlike you, I don't dream of a mythic return. Because, unlike you, I'm not a paragon of faithlessness.

Because, unlike you, I have something I believe in.

***

Thanks to my innate curiosity, interest, and help from some enlightened others, I broadened my viewpoint. Then, the epiphany became a state of being; I lived in a constant state of observation and realization. The world lay open before me, and I connected the dots, connected the strands of thought and belief and ideology, to slowly reveal shards of reality.

The reason America disapproves of this, the reason why America would rather hold on to a flimsy supermarket idealism, is because reality is too much for this country.

Do I not love my country, then? Am I not a patriot?

I am, but I have realized that I cannot join America in her disjointed dreams. Rather, I must bring America with me, out of the delusions it remains sunken in.

That fellow Plato, a famous Greek philosopher, gave a very solid example once of people who had spent their entire lives inside a cave. They did not know of reality outside their cave; they had only ever seen shadows. One day a man amongst them walked out of the cave, and was amazed by the colors and forms and beauty he saw. Excited, he returned to the cave, telling his friends about the world outside. All they had to do was turn away from the cave wall and go outside. But what did his friends do? They rejected him! They rejected him because he came bearing unfamiliar ideas, concepts that simply did not match their paradigm. The paradigm of the cave is all they had ever known, and thus, they told the man that he was mad.

Any man who has seen beyond the paradigm knows that life beyond it is better. There is a whole world outside of the cave. There is a whole reality begging to be seen. Yet within the cave, our whole entire country is busy playing a game of chess in the dark. But here, in the darkness of the cave, we see only black and white; we do not see the nuances of the pieces. We cannot distinguish the real game being played. The real game can only be seen and played outside of the paradigm; only then can you tell which piece is the King. Only then can you see who wins and who loses.

The ignorance of the masses is for the convenience of the powerful. Those who have created the construct are unwilling to 'pass the mic' to anyone who can speak contrary to their narrative. Look at the way media works today: it's an echo chamber of the same constant, regurgitated idiocy, the same ideologies spewed over and over until they enter the public norm. It is a conscious attempt to turn the cultural zeitgeist into a veritable modern gospel. Their ultimate desire is to create a society that harbors no epiphany – a perfect cage that allows no peeking at the world outside.

To receive an epiphany is not an idle process.

One does not arrive to it by mistake or without effort. The seeds of knowledge must be sown into the mind through willful search, curiosity, and an active desire to know more. Knowledge must be gained, earned. But if the people, the American people, are lost in a perpetual dream, how would they ever search? And this is what our modern media, politics, and entertainment offer. Dreams. The American dream didn't just turn into a nightmare; it became slowly apparent to the dreamers that they were locked inside. There is no escape from the American dream because it is designed to be a wall of alternating indoctrination and distraction.

Are we surprised that this country is a host of so

many mental conditions? Are we surprised that the average American citizen feels so anxious and alienated?

This country and its oligarchs have taken faith out of the equation. They have left the vestiges of broken, tattered rituals in the space once reserved for faith; they have left empty churches and individualist half-faiths behind to appease the hopeless. But true faith, true belief, always demands the truth. It demands reality.

When Christ preached against the moneylenders, did He simply sit and talk against them? No, he went and upended the stalls of the moneylenders. True faith is always destructive in some capacity; it tears apart the established order, the status quo, and reveals the injustices in society.

Christ was not just a religious figure; He was a social reformer. He arrived in this world as a man to create an example for the people. He aimed to create a clear precedent for mankind in general to follow. It is not enough for this country to consider what is good or bad – what we need is conviction and the will to look beyond the comfortable lie to see the hard truth.

What America needs is an epiphany of its own. For years, this country has eaten out of the hands of the very moneylending class Jesus challenged – the class of rich, privileged Jewish people that today identify themselves as the Zionists. Any challenge against this class is branded racial in nature; any question leveled at them is labeled as fragrant anti-semitism. Yet this realization does not dawn upon the American people because, slowly, the mere thought of criticizing these people has become taboo in this country. The color construct has created such an impenetrable wall around these people that it becomes impossible for many to look past it – but look past it we must.

What is fair must be commended, and what is wrong must be known to be wrong. Perhaps that is the most basic, simple epiphany needed for this country: the realization that the truth must be said, even if it's unpleasant... especially if it's unpleasant. Inconvenient truths might irk the rotten upper crust of this country, but recognizing them is vital if this country is to survive the biblical deluge of its own failings.

***

That day on the road, when I felt the utterance of Genesis come upon me, was also an epiphany. For the first time in my life, I felt the strong bond that connected me to my Creator; for the first time, I felt true faith, as powerful and terrible as the understanding was.

Every realization that gives something also takes something away. The exchange is not always equivalent, but its existence is above doubt – it is always a transaction of sorts. Generally, what one loses is the bliss of ignorance, but let me ask you: how useful is this blissful euphoria if you're drowning but unaware of your situation? How useful is sitting in your room as it fills up with water up to your neck, with you sitting there pretending everything is fine?

Though it appears at first that knowledge is a curse and ignorance a blessing, this is simply so at face value – in reality, it is the opposite. Even though knowledge is painful, it is the path to longer and more lasting satisfaction. This, too, is a realization that strikes many too late because knowledge is inevitable – in this world, bliss cannot last. The dream is fragile; it will always break. This world was never meant for delusions, only the starkest of reality.

And so, there is no escape. What matters, though, is when you have this unfortunate epiphany – and whether you still have enough time to do something about it.

***

The final chain of epiphany I'll cover here is about identity.

When I realized that we aren't 'black', I realized how meaningful our roots are. When I realized this, I did my research and concluded that we are the African Descendants of Slaves. But then I considered what that meant and what, then, should be important to us.

We are the descendants of slaves that had everything torn from them – and what is left for someone with everything torn from them? What was left for Adam and his progeny when we fell from Eden? Faith – ultimately, all that's left is faith. This faith is what America lacks; so many supposedly holy men are charlatans, and so many supposedly religious politicians are content to quote scripture without the slightest idea of the depth the words hold. Religion in America is mostly symbolic in nature; it is so weak that it lacks even a paradigm of its own, instead ramshackle in with other paradigms such as the 'Great America' delusion.

    This country, like all of God's children, needs His wisdom; yet, ADS in particular have been made to stray from His proper word. Though many hear the sermons, the verses and even parrot them, it is purposeless – the true purpose and message behind the text is lost. The context is lost. The very meaning is lost.

    If the American Descendants of Slaves, and indeed, if this country is going to create a future worth living, we must return to the roots of faith. We must return to the text with a new context; we must return with the intention to not just read but rather understand the–

B.I.B.L.E.

*"When you read **God's Word**, you must constantly be sayingto yourself, "It is talking **to me**, and **about me**."*

Soren Kierkegaard.

I have done my best to be true to God in this life.

When I have called Him, it has always been from a place of truth, a place of honesty, a place free from unthinking ritual or petty desire. My call to the divine has generally been spiritual in nature, carefully unselfish, because that is what I believe – too many people have simply used faith as a way to deal with their material, mundane problems. Not enough have ever bothered to look deeper.

Where to look deeper, you ask? Why, look at the source – look at the Bible, or better yet, look at the B.I.B.L.E. Now, what does that mean?

B.I.B.L.E. is an acronym for what the holy book stands for:

"Believers use these Instructions to gain

understanding Before they Leave their temporary confinement on Earth."

The reason for this acronym is that it reveals the truth behind the scripture. The understanding of the Bible is meant for the hereafter. Religion, faith, and spirituality, by very definition, are tied to spirituality, to the world beyond, and to the kingdom come. The world we live in today is a fallen thing, a detour, a pit confining Adam's progeny. Yet we have somehow managed to take this temporary confinement and turn it into an entire playground of restrictive paradigms. We have put even more gates and walls within our prison; we have strengthened our chains.

Instead of seeing it as a historical artifact, or a by-the-numbers book, always assume that the text of the Bible is being actively said unto you. Always assume that the text is written for you, because it was — it is a guide. Too often, humans will deflect their sins to others — we will tell ourselves that there are sinners worse than us, people more deserving of the biblical chastisement than poor old us. Many presume their innocence when they are, in fact, guilty — in fact, all of us are!

This is a world where innocence cannot endure

from the moment you lose your childhood, you lose the precious last vestiges of the natural, Edenic innocence that had remained within you, a vestigial connection to the life Adam and Eve had once lived. This is a tainted existence, yet we have decided it to be pure — we have decided ourselves to be pure. And so mankind spends time trying to justify its sins, excesses, wars, and mistakes.

Is America not the best example of this? Has she not justified her mistakes over and over? Has this country not justified every atrocity, every crime, and every abhorrent choice made by the POTUS (President of The United States) or the various other construct-strengthened institutions that run this dystopian state? America is constructed around the idea of presumed innocence, the idea that we are simply playing into a manifest destiny. Yet, the horrific thread of the American Dream was not spun by God – it was spun in dark offices and shadowy corners, right under the bright facades of our offices.

The truth is clear, but we shy away because we can't bear the burden of our own dishonesty.

***

You may notice another element in the acronym B.I.B.L.E. that does not jump out at first glance – the idea that this world is not only temporary but also a place of confinement.

Now, why is this important? It is important because it demonstrates that Adam's fall was not only a change in levels, status, or grace. It was a fall into place he could not escape from, from a place he could never return to. It depicts the totality of consequence – the idea that consequence can never be reversed. Even though this state of being in this world is temporary, we cannot reach salvation by going backward; we can only move forward.

The Bible demonstrates that the human experience is unequivocally linear. Even if God above can see and perceive things in a way that is completely beyond our understanding, we ourselves will only ever perceive events and time, cause and consequence, and futures and histories with the same lens of linearity. We will always see one thing happen, then another, and then another.

Due to this state of being, we are confined. Now, confinement isn't a pleasant experience – and for a large part, neither is living on this rock! All around us, a thousand evils raise their head every day, and they have for centuries. Eons. The Bible itself chronicles the evils of man; it tells all the terrible atrocities humankind has done in this world. There was no period of true purity, true righteousness, or true brilliance in the history of mankind as we know it.

But in America, the evil has intensified – because it has been sanctioned. And when even those who are meant to guide their flocks start leading them astray, most of your average preachers and denominations simply cannot be trusted. What you can trust, however, is the text itself – unaltered, true, and pure.

Yet many cannot keep their faith. Even the once faithful lose their sense of religious identity when surrounded by evils and impotent religious officials parading depraved icons in churches.

Many simply disavow religion. But then, stepping out on the street, they see the carnage of America today – they see men fighting like dogs for survival, climbing and clawing and screaming for a spot on the social ladder, mired in constructs and paradigms, lost to all rational thought and sanity.

And when a man sees that, unedited, unfiltered, there truly is no going back for him. Like me, after my realization in Louisville, he loses his last vestige of innocence and can never again return.

***

It's no surprise, then, that when the average American reads the Bible, he or she is looking for solace or comfort to help with the hellscape that is the world outside. Even if it acts as a cheap opiate to temporarily calm their frayed nerves.

But they miss the point – they miss the real purpose of the text.

The Bible was not meant to give you earthly comfort; it was meant to give you a glimpse into the Truth. It is a set of instructions, a toolkit for epiphanies. And the truth, as we have discussed, is always destructive in some capacity – yet understanding is better than the alternative. Truth is better than the alternative. The bitterness of honesty is better than the sweet bile of lies.

But Uncle Me'Shorn, you ask, what's the point of gaining this sort of understanding if the ultimate purpose is to move on from this world anyways?

Because that's the purpose. We spend our lives here wondering why we exist, why we are here, and why we must live in this world. But the truth is that we only exist to know the why of things. We exist to try and look beyond the curtain, to look back and forward, to see the past and present, and to chart the course of the human experience like sailors on a voyage. This life is temporary. It is fleeting. What matters is the mode by which we enter eternity and what we bring with us then. The good, the decent, and the wise are who are rewarded by the system of divinity – not the dividers nor the hypocrites.

Thus, religion is intrinsically a living process. The Bible is a living book that calls to our souls and helps us see a world, a reality, hidden behind the veil of our mundane existence. It is the process of peering beyond the white noise of mediocrity and urbanity and letting your spirit rise about the confines of your flesh. To have faith means to transcend.

Yet, faith in this country has manifested in the opposite direction. Instead of transcending the material boundaries of our mortal existence, it has descended into it; the faith that was meant to be a helpline to heaven has fallen into the pit right with us. The anchor has gone adrift; the center is uncentered. We have lost something essential here

the liveliness and vitality of a living faith. What is left is a false paragon, a deadened mockery of religion that calls out meaningless slogans and is preached by paunchy old Europeans and race-construct-indoctrinated African Americans.

From once being invaluable, religion has now fallen to the status of being a transaction.

But all is not lost – because although this matrix has been created to obscure the truth, the Bible remains with us. The guidelines remain with us. The truth may be hidden, its natural veil even further hidden, but the path to the truth is manifest.

To my fellow Americans and Descendants of Slaves, Uncle Me'Shorn says: "Read the Bible, and know that it is the B.I.B.L.E."

***

Religion in this country is not only underrepresented and marginalized – it has been actively perverted and misused for political agendas.

Faithless preachers, ignorant demagogues, and lying politicians have defiled the purity of faith.

Christianity has unfortunately been used to prop up and justify some of the worst decisions and atrocities made by this country. America has fooled her men and women to go fight her wars, ostensibly in the name of 'God, country, and the American way', while all the conflict is about is power and wealth for a chosen few.

And thus, there must be a cleansing. Faith must

be reclaimed and purified from the wretched state it has been left in. Faith in the American context must be unlearned, so that true faith can be relearned.

And so, we must stand firm for our faith. We must stand true and resolute in the face of all that is thrown at us. Ultimately, we must call out those who continue to misuse religion for their own gains. We must call out those who claim to be godly men only for their own purposes.

We must call out the architects of the–

American Faith.

> *"If there can be anything more **diametrically opposed** to the religion of **Jesus**, than the working of this **soul-killing system** ... we wish to be shown where it can be found."*

Sojourner Truth.

As we discussed, religion in America suffers from a problem – and this problem is modern America itself. Something in this country consistently denies faith. Something in the heart of America has broken and has broken the vitality of religion alongside it.

And so, faith – true faith, at least – has been replaced by a semi-functional, bastardized American Faith, an amalgamation and corruption of various facets of religion, social trauma, and the dystopian reality we currently inhabit. The American Faith is a funny thing – simultaneously rigid and fanatical while also lacking any basic idea of the religion it seeks to represent! Very little out there is as unchristian as the brand of Christianity propagated in this country through television sermons and self-styled, popular preachers with as much moral integrity as unthinking social media influencers.

The liberalization of faith has subverted the very essence of it; all faith, all religion is rooted in the fiber of tradition. It is rooted in the idea that things matter, that the text matters, and that there must be space for true, unashamed faith in any society or system. Yet this is untrue of the American experience. Here, religion has been relegated to a peripheral status, watered down, and handed around without any standards. There is no minimal entry into the American faith. There is no social vitality. There is nothing to tell whether the religious worship is true or whether the words of worship come from the heart or not.

Until I spoke in tongues that night on the road, I had been honest enough to never speak the words of the Bible without faith. Yet, why is it that I never felt that connection to faith before that moment? Why is it that, living in this country, I never felt that strong pull toward the purity of religion? Let Uncle Me'Shorn tell you why: because the American Faith is essentially soulless. It is founded on the idea of religion without understanding, faith without truth, and sermons without scripture. It is, as said prior, a transaction; you put in your prayers and receive temporary comfort.

This temporary nature of the comfort received from the modern church is a sign, a symptom.

Nothing holy is temporary; all that God promises in the Bible is everlasting. The only reason the solace offered by the modern church is temporary is because it belongs to a worldly paradigm; temporariness as a trait is uniquely mortal. Our lives are temporary; our stay in this world is similarly transient. God and His kingdom bring a lasting joy, not a momentary respite.

The dots connect; the outcome is clear.

There is nothing godly in this peripheral faith.

***

This cold, crude, and materialistic way of looking at religion is very classically American – but where did it come from?

The religious bedrock of the Slaves our kinfolk descend from has always been alive, very involved, and very focused on truth, wisdom, and respect.

This almost dead-eyed, clinical faith is alien to us

but so is it alien to the 'white man'! The European settlers who came to the Americas, for all their flaws, were puritans, deeply spiritual ones. For all the flaws of the extreme strictness of their faith and practices, the last thing they were was indulgent.

Yet today, faith is an afterthought in America. It is an institution. Churches have devolved into therapy clinics for those who lack the means to go to an actual therapist; faith has ceased to be a spiritual anchor and has thus devolved into becoming nothing more than a social institution, like the sad asylums that once housed the mentally challenged.

    This businesslike, commodified view of religion does, however, have a purpose. It strengthens the constructs we have because, on its own, religion itself is a paradigm – or is meant to be. By making it a pastime, one leaches all vitality and life from the concept, making other constructs powerful enough to consume and replace it. Any explanation for the weakness of the religious paradigm in America that doesn't consider the possibility of an agenda is bogus; there is nothing natural or organic about the roughshod, muddy version of religion this country stands on.

    This once-clear pool of faith has been sullied by an agenda, and there is little doubt as to the origins. The origins are that little state in the middle east that this country has protected for so many years. I mean, of course, the state of Israel – and already, I can feel as though I have broken a taboo by stating the name! Yet it is true; the businesslike, unsentimental, and cold faith proliferating our societies is directly connected to a Judaic narrative – the narrative of the construct.

    Where religion demands understanding, deceptive paradigms and constructs aim to cloud and obscure. The Matrix created by these paradigms is the antithesis of the Biblical thesis – it is the opposite of the truth, being falsehood incarnate. This matrix defers the importance of religion by deferring the reality of the impermanence of this life; by tying the anchor of the American public down to material needs, desires, and commodities, the matrix successfully creates a deference that never stops. There is always one more day, always one more thing to buy, always one last sin, always one last lie.

And thus, we are too late to the Truth – because we thought it'd keep waiting. The Zionist has thus created two bubbles – one is a bubble made of constructs to keep us out, and the other is a bubble designed to keep us in. This second bubble is the matrix, a labyrinth that this country wanders in, lost and delayed.

The American Dream/Nightmare is not American at all: It is very much a manufactured product designed with clear intent. And it is not like it's possible to speak out; the first, defensive bubble is still active. Even infamous figures and celebrities like Kanye West instantly lose wealth, fame, and credibility if they publicly question or are in any way vocal against this invisible hegemony. It is, in many ways, the perfect shield.

The Judaic narrative is cloaked in and protected by the race construct; from being a religious persuasion, the Jewish faith suddenly turns into the archetypical Semitic race if threatened. Say anything against the political and hegemonic threat posed by the religious impurities spread by Zionists, and suddenly you are branded racist! This racial identification to faith is utterly alien to Christianity, and indeed, all Abrahamic faiths – even Judaism itself! The Zionist agenda has everything to do with power, the consolidation of resources, and control over every domain in this country.

And so, the race-faith dichotomy is a reality in America. Only here is there Black Christianity and White Christianity, White Jesus and Black Jesus; we as a country, Lord forgive us, have divided the very essence of His faith on the basis of the melanin in our skin, the identities we have scrounged, the lies we have told ourselves. Thus, religion loses all of its power to unite, inspire, strengthen, and draw people together. It instead turns into something else entirely – a tool to divide and break apart. And now our churches wage a narrative war against each other; racist 'white churches' and self-victimizing 'black churches' continue the song and dance, dragging the narratives of racism and segregation into the 21st Century, long after they should have died down.

Out of all the terrible things I experienced in my childhood because of my mother's negligence, the best consequence of this upbringing was that she kept me away from the communal 'black churches'. Thus I escaped the indoctrination they enacted on many others, and even though I had a phase of my life when I wasn't so awake, I was never completely lulled and brainwashed into believing every construct-strengthening word that came out of some pastor's mouth.

I don't doubt that many in these churches believe what they preach – but their ignorance is no excuse. To come into the world is to have lost the bliss of heaven in any case – to try and cling to it now is a mistake, especially if it drags other people down the wrong road as well.

If you are a pastor or preacher of American Christianity, pause – halt your sermon, America. Analyze it. Look into the heart of the paradigms you endorse. Look into the heart of what you are saying. Look at your beliefs, and examine them in the light of day, with reference to the actual text you claim to stand for. Read, and then read again – and perhaps then, you will begin to see an inkling of the truth, and the truth is that you have been laboring in the night for no gain. You have been working in the dark to spread it even further; you have been blinded by the deceptive paradigms that have consumed you.

***

The black churches of this country have developed their own practices in time that have deviated from the practices of the actual Christian tradition.

Many elements of these new practices are derived from practices from African spiritualism – but unrealized. These half-remembered ideas had no strength on their own to sustain faith, belief, or hope and, instead, were used by slaves and their descendants to supplement and strengthen the extant faith they found some comfort in. Do I understand this? I do! But I neither understand nor condone how these practices have turned into an echo chamber of 'blackness'; these half- remembered tribal practices are futile nostalgia, a futile attempt to reconnect with the past. But the past and human heritage don't exist to be escaped into. They exist to serve as warning, guidelines, and a place to trace your progress from. The attempt to return to their lost origins is a fallacy that many of America's black have fallen to, and have led themselves and their flocks into a fruitless abyss of self-pity.

To reiterate the example of the story I told earlier about the Buddha; if we are to pour anything pure or wholesome into a vessel, we must ensure that the vessel itself is clean, or else it may taint whatever enters into it. This happened to 'Black' Christianity; the peoples who came here as alienated slaves were still full of prior practices and ideologies that simply could not mesh with Christianity.

Add to this the mess of self-identification, and all knowledge that the colored churches came across has become distorted by the color-lens they could not shake away. And thus, 'black religion' was lost in a path of constant, unrealized nostalgia.

But instead of trying to cling to or hide from various aspects of the past, we, the descendants of slaves, must acknowledge the existence of the past and continue to move forward. This is the only way; we must transcend the limitations we have found ourselves embroiled in. We must transcend the American faith, for it is intrinsically the path to faithlessness. It is a hollow tunnel that leads nowhere, promising the world and delivering shadows. And like blind men in the dark, the American people stumble around in it, unable to feel or connect with each other, instead striking each other with flailing limbs and cursing.

And there can be no unity in a place of darkness.

The truth is that the American faith must be moved past or otherwise dispelled; the darkness must be parted as Moses parted the Red sea. It is ironic that from the people who passed from this parted sea, arose the descendant generations of Zion who have drowned and trapped this country like they were once trapped, between the Pharaoh and the deep blue sea. And now, as plague and poverty and horror descends on this once-new continent, it is at the hands of a manufactured faith.

When Cain killed Abel and was asked by God about his brother's whereabouts, he carelessly tossed the phrase: "Am I my brother's keeper?" God never answered him, but the lack of an answer is also interesting. This selfish line of thinking has been echoed in America by the so-called 'oppressed minorities' proliferating the neighborhoods and markets – the Judaic narrative and the false American dream followed by immigrants continue to serve a selfish and thoroughly materialistic agenda. There is no care, no love, no understanding in this new American faith; there are only disinterested parties profiting from others' miseries. When questioned about their behavior, they answer with a familiar question:

"Am I my brother's keeper?"

***

In America, the liberal democratic party has particularly profited from this self-serving style of 'independent', 'individualistic' Christianity. It has continued to sell it as a package with a perverted version of the humanist values this country was founded on, emphasizing 'personal freedom' above all else – as though a man could ever be totally free, as though they themselves aren't attempting to capture the people in the constructs of their making. Is it any surprise that the people of this country are so over-programmed and indoctrinated?

This false construct of global Christianity has deceived and created an unnatural system of pseudo-faith that can not be reversed by new behavior and true believers. The tainted, divisive, and corrupt forms of Christianity that this country abides by must be unlearned. The American people must make a stand – they must unlearn the tragic shambles of faith they have grown up in.

Only then can the truth be relearned, pure and untarnished.

And this is why Uncle Me'Shorn stands for no color. I stand for no race. I stand for God and His people, no matter the color of their skin. No matter what, I truly believe that before Him, all lives are the same, be they of a Prince or a Pauper, Man or Woman, Innocent or a Sinner.

I don't believe that 'white lives matter' or 'black lives matter'.

All I know, is that—

God's Lives Matter.

"There is neither Jew nor Greek, there is neither slave nor free, there is no male and female, for you are all one in ChristJesus."

Galatians 3:28.

God's Lives Matter, or GLM, is what I believe in. Uncle Me'Shorn isn't compelled by race, or color, or the plethora of petty constructs that motivate the rest of the people. If I am to stand for something, if I am to believe in something, it must be something nobler than the skin, truer than the flawed bodies we inhabit. God's Lives Matter is a conceptual understanding and collection of principles influenced by Rev. Sun Myung Moon.

And this idea is what compels me and all others who put their faith in GLM: the idea that God's love doesn't discriminate. It doesn't segregate. It doesn't whitewash or black-wash – it is undivided, all-embracing. God is not petty; He is not caught up in the mortal mess of Paradigms.

The lives we live originate, ultimately, not in a lost Eden, but in God Himself. Although we talk of Adam and his fall, Adam himself was never the origin

– he may be the origin of our Earthly existence, but our immortal souls, our lives all come from God. And they are, indeed, His.

As a movement, GLM attempts to defeat the deceptive paradigms talked about – it aims to transcend the limitations put upon us by the arch-paradigm, the terrible matrix-construct that has constantly and consistently shackled us and subverted the fabric of America. The movement ultimately aims to bring a message, not of hate-mongering or finger-pointing, but of general love for humanity. All of God's lives matter, and I mean all; America likes to play an importance game as various groups and peoples and ethnicities compete for more 'relevance' in the media, but to God, there is no difference. Man is man, no matter what he identifies as.

There are so many who have been marginalized and disenfranchised within the American society, people with no voices, no one to stand for them, no family. These are people who have been silenced, people who have had their constitutional rights trodden over, told to stay quiet or face consequences. Because that's how America works – either people bite the carrot, or learn to fear the stick.

But it doesn't have to be like this. It shouldn't be like this. The American Believer of the 21st century must learn that he is not alone; that there is a group of believers that see him for who his is, not for the color of his skin. A group that is intent on moving past all social divisions segregating the people of the

Lord by sex, religion, color, race, property, wealth, education, or disability. The 'Great' America we live in, layered as it is in constructs, promotes a soulless, isolationist system of being that is actively ruining the very concept of a national and global community. The anarchic system we see at work in our lives, our elections, even our geo-politics, is all driven by people wearing the mask of Cain, smiling that careless smile as they trod over their brothers.

The only way forward, then, is through building something. It is easy to destroy. It is easy to try and break down everything you disagree with, easy to try and ruin everything that you find wrong or evil or corrupt. But although the very fabric of this country has been corrupted by those with power and privilege, your Uncle Me'Shorn still hopes and believes.

And what do I hope for? What do I believe in?

I hope for an America that can right its path. I hope for an America that can see and recognize the mistakes it has made, the mistakes it's in the process of making. I hope for an America that can stop looking back, and start looking forward. And like MLK, I too hope for an America where the segregation of races may finally come to an end.

But hopes are nothing without the will to turn them into reality. They are nothing without the power of belief. And I believe in moving forward and building instead of destroying. As William Boetcker put it, "You cannot strengthen the weak by weakening the strong... You cannot further the brotherhood of man by inciting class hatred." Though paradigms and constructs must certainly be challenged, targeting individuals or groups must remain off the table. Any change that we bring should be made with the idea of creating a net positive; if equality is brought at the expense of tearing everyone else down, it is an injustice in and of itself.

If we are to be unified, we must rise united.

***

Instead of shouting out 'black lives matter' or 'white lives matter', isn't it wiser to look at the terrible consequences of this sort of thinking?

Has it not created divisions among us? Among our states, neighborhoods, even our households? Even parents and children have become divided over this futile war, when in truth, the task was in front of us this whole time: to move beyond this childish dichotomy and try and make something true and real.

Whatever slogan people in this country choose to support, they do so inevitably at the cost of the others; no one from BLM will ever say that police lives matters. To choose a specific group to support and represent is to automatically exclude everyone else.

This 'choice' is as blatant a construct as you'll ever see, just as there is no doubt in my mind that all lives matter to God. Your Uncle Me'Shorn can say this without hesitation. All men and women have their own honor; all of mankind has a right to respect.

The dignity of man is his right as the viceroy of the Lord on his earth; every soul has this right, for every soul is the recipient of His love.

Christ was not the Christ of the Jews, nor was He the Lord of the Greeks; neither did he bear his message only to the poor, nor only the rich.

He came unto this would to save all of mankind, regardless of gender or creed or caste.

***

The Lord doesn't play favorites – but humans certainly do. Humans continue to try to divide themselves into tribes and castes; they continue to try to create difference, which intrinsically creates the path to claiming superiority.

This desire for superiority, like all other desire, is the true root of conflict. Desire is the heart of the issue; it is the heart of America's woes. This country is a children's playground, a veritable wonderland, designed to fulfill every desire and craving. Life matters less here than commodities, and by God, everything here is a commodity – America has perfected material consumerism. We live in a society where people don't live the life God gave unto them; instead, they consume all the products they can.

The American need to over-consume has created a culture of gluttony; the health issues in this country are obvious to any onlooker. Gluttony is and has always been an American sin, compared to other countries around the world, and the overindulgence of our people is a waste of the lives we live. The people keep chanting white lives matter or black lives matter, but in truth, American lives barely matter. If they mattered, would people not take better care of them? If they mattered, they wouldn't be wasted eating junk, collecting worthless things, and spending all our time laboring for superfluous products.

We need to realize that we aren't just living 'our lives'. We aren't just living lives that intrinsically belong to us. Life is a gift, not permission to indulge in the only-live-once brand of hedonism this country loves to peddle. It is a gift, and like all gifts, it was given. The lives we live are God's, and should be cared for accordingly. If someone gives you something as a gift, you don't throw it around carelessly or knowingly tear it down – these are basic manners.

The people must grow conscious of the fact that human lives are lived on borrowed time – they are colorless, clear and beautiful as glass.

There is no division in life itself – there is no life that matters more than others. There is no hierarchy of human experience, and that's the beauty of it. Everything matters, or as the essential truth of God's Lives Matter goes: "Every human life created by God has infinite value."

***

After my spiritual rebirth and my remarriage in 1996, I gave thanks to my Creator. At this point I was still living in West End, and one day, in an honest conversation to my Creator, I spoke unto God and said, if you can bring me home, I would be absolutely blessed.

Then I heard a message in my head say unto me:

"I ain't released you yet."

As unbelievable as it sounds, I promised you, reader, that I heard these words. In that moment, Uncle Me'Shorn felt a burst of inspiration within my soul – I stopped as if time had stopped. Then I looked down at myself. I was wearing a T-Shirt that said "ARMY".

Inspiration struck.

I ran home and wrote down something, paused, and took a look at what I had written. The paper said the phrase I had just heard – then I changed it. Now the paper read:

"God Ain't Released Me Yet."

In other words, G.A.R.M.Y.

I later located an attorney and trademark it; but I didn't do anything with it until now. Whether in America or globally, God Ain't Released Me (nor you) Yet – as we are the soldiers and servant serving in God's ARMY.

And that is G.A.R.M.Y.

The GLM campaign is to inspire, encourage, and create alliances with other believers who have also received their epiphany. Like the Wise Men who left their home, family and life to fulfilled their purpose, many have felt the call to follow the message – and I am one of you souls who have felt the burden of responsibility when faced with the state of the modern world. We must break away from the ruins of lost innocence, trudge past the cavernous echoes of dysfunctional families, and stand there in the harsh light of truth, for the first time seeing the ever-flickering, half invisible constructs and paradigm that have ensnared, divided, and conquered western civilization.

America, like Rome and Judea of old, has lost her path – and when a civilization loses its path, it must be fixed, lest it collapse. In the 21st century, that terrible onus of responsibility falls upon us true believers, we who received epiphany. The blame for the state of the world may not fall upon us, but it surely will if we sit idle in the midst of a collapse. Destiny harkens, and we must answer.

The GLM campaign is a companion to Reminder, Witness, and Revealer, R.W. R.; it is the confirmation that we are the descendants of Adam and Eve who lost their innocence in the garden. No longer are we the innocent sparrows provided for by the Lord. No, we can and must create new wisdom, opportunities, responsibilities, respect, and knowledge – we must obey the laws of W.O.R.K. This it the curse that Man must bear – and either he can choose to ignore it in a bliss of false paradigms, or face them like he is meant to.

We, the Fallen that were once innocent, can never return to that state – and so, it's extremely important Parent-Gods do not alter Children's innocence through unnatural, dysfunctional behaviors.

On earth, we are all called to become our brothers and sisters' Keepers. When Cain sarcastically said, "Am I my brother's keeper?" God did not answer. Abel's life mattered, just as all lives matter – to save the life of one is to save a life given by God, and to take it or trivialize it is sacrilegious. Every life matters and must discover itself through discovering love and overcoming the world.

***

When we realize that God's lives matter, we realize that there was never any difference between materiality and spirituality to begin with.

For years, the material / spiritual split has divided intellectuals; the two have been seen as separate spheres of existence, constantly clashing. Material systems have considered pure spirituality to be useless or simply impractical, while on the other hand, spirituality has always held a similarly dim view of raw materialism. Yet this barrier dividing the two is flimsy – there is not a 'world above' and a 'world below'; spirituality and material existence are parts of the same whole, two sides of the same coin. The lives we live are not material things separate from spiritual existence.

We live in the spirit; the existence we experience is not purely physical. Even despite the traumas and the sufferings of the earth, it is the spirit that endures; even though we can never return back to the state we fell from, spiritually, we are still connected to those roots. It is this realization that proves that the lives we live are not so different; the very experience of being alive is proof that we are more than our skin and our bones. We are not the melanin in our skin; we are neither black nor white. The color construct, or any construct, has no impact on the nature of the spirit, because a human life is the essential unit of being; although perceptions can be twisted this way or that, the truth remains the same.

And that is what God's Lives Matter is about – the truth. Finding it and knowing it in your heart. The paradigms and constructs that seek to deceive the mind and heart play to a tribalism; they prey on the aspect of human desire. But desire is ultimately selfish – in truth, responsibility is the mark of a steadfast man. As the Divine Principles teach, a man must live for the sake of others. Living for oneself is inevitably flawed, because living for oneself leads to a path of excuses and self-delusions. A human isolated from other humans will have no priorities, no path, no goal, no real aim – an individual this isolated will inevitably be an ostracized soul, easily affected by outside, deceptive paradigms, because he has nothing else to give him meaning.

But we must ignore the construct. Ignore their lies. Stand for the truth, for what matters: life, joy, truth, and love. Do your W.O.R.K – pull your weight. Do your best to do what you can for your friends, for your communities, for your–

Part IV
Families

The Future Family.

"The strength of a family, like the strength of an army, lies inits loyalty to each other."

Mario Puzo.

When I was young, my experience of family was – well, as you've read, dysfunctional would perhaps be putting it mildly. It was a childhood that took a toll on my very soul, and had disastrous consequences for the rest of my life. For a long time, I felt only pain and self-revulsion as I continued to live in my childhood home – as the innocence was stripped from my consciousness, I grew aware of my family's nature.

It is a moment of terrible disillusionment when a child sees the parent-god come to earth in as catastrophic a fall as I saw. The idol created within the mind cracks and collapses, and the faith you once had in your family is wrenched away from you. For anyone who has been a part of a dysfunctional or abusive childhood, you know exactly what I mean; many lose faith in family overall as an institution. Many distance themselves and cut off all human contact, fearful of ending up back in that terrible situation.

The truth about trauma is that it is not just 'chemicals in the brain', as some people like to put it nowadays – trauma is like a scar across your back, in a spot you cannot reach. It is like a wound you can never put a true salve on; all you can do is wait for it to hopefully scab over. But trauma is also not an individualistic experience; it is always a fluid thing with a place in wider society. Trauma often passes from individual to individual – it is the means by which the initial innocence of man is depleted and torn. Trauma is the gaping wound left behind by the loss of innocence – and unsurprisingly, the most common form of trauma is familial trauma.

Familial trauma can, if left unchecked, result in generational trauma – which is to say, the sins of the father not just affecting, but possessing the son. While we all bear the scars of our past, we must do our best not to let it dominate us – we must hold onto our roots from a distance, with the awareness to not repeat the same mistakes made by our own families. And this is what I have always believed in; the way I grew up, I swore to myself that I would never repeat the same atmosphere in my own house. I would never give a place or hearth to the degenerate, unnatural behaviors I saw under that roof.

Me'Shorn T. Daniels swore to never repeat the cycle.

***

Only when a man can look past and grow beyond

his past family can he consider the future family. What does that mean, you ask? The future family is a combination of two concepts – the very concept of the family in the future, and the way a man conceptualizes it personally. In other words, the future family means both the idea of the family in the future, as well as the way a man might imagine it for himself.

The family in America is a slowly dying institution. Over the past century, American households are losing control over their children, over their means, over their desires, their aims, and even their own identities. The family is traditionally tied to gender roles, and over time, those have certainly collapsed in America – the very idea of having clearly differentiated gender roles is offensive to many. The relative simplicity of what should be a family has been lost in a sea of diversity endorsed by those in power.

I've seen how constructs have distorted families – those who have accepted being America's black have normalized a culture of absentee parenthood, dissociated father figures disappearing just as their child comes into the world. Single mothers clutching children from multiple fathers, desperate for cash – this is not a healthy family. This is not culture. This is a problem – and a problem that is affecting the poor children in question. A family exists to stop this sort of behavior from developing, but as the familial institution crumbles, this sort of behavior grows ever-more commonplace.

Once, morality and values were in the hands of the familial institution, but now, children consume them directly from media – media which is heavily doctored and designed to produce a certain result. Children find themselves consuming media at a breakneck pace, unregulated by their parents, unseen, unchecked, and much of this media contains messaging designed by those in power.

The future family in general, if one is to be a pessimist, is a toothless institution. At worst, one can even perceive America's current socio-cultural turmoil to be a hotbed for dysfunctional family structures that can create a chain of trauma for years to come.

But your Uncle Me'Shorn is not a pessimist. I refuse to look only at the dark – I refuse to lose myself to resignation and hopelessness.

I believe that there is hope. As long as people continue to have faith in a functional caring family, there is hope. As long as people continue to believe in a family where the parent-god persists, where a man and woman can truly be there for each other, there is hope yet; as long as the ideals of married life continue to be followed, there is hope. The most important role played by a family is perhaps support – a family's purpose is to support every member, lifting them up instead of pulling them down. In an age of terrible uncertainty, the family should be the bedrock for a man to build himself on – instead of running off on wives and cheating, a man in these times should be a man who is willing to commit to his family.

Its either that, or be lost to the encroaching chaos, because there certainly is a terror on the horizon. What matters is whether we succumb to it, or whether we fight against it — and I believe in the second, the harder choice. There is nothing good about accepting defeat. To accept defeat is to accept the lack of a future — any future. The future is built by the individuals who are children today, and if uncared for, what sort of future will they make?

Each house, each family needs a figurehead — but if it continues to be acceptable for our men to act in fickle, unmanly ways, how could our families hope to stand? If we continue to tolerate irresponsibility, who will suffer except society itself? If we continue to invite overly liberal, even depraved ideologies into our homes, the consequences will be such that your Uncle Me'Shorn doesn't even want to think about it. I've lived through one such childhood — to see it replicated across America is something I honestly never wish to see.

To all those who are reading this book — above all the deceptive constructs, the problematic paradigms, the issues and paradoxes and revelations, the most important thing is to be the best you can be for your family. Be their bedrock — and be an agent of change, if required. We must all bear our burdens, and holding a family together is one of them. Both man and woman must contribute equally for a family to work; there must be harmony and synchronicity among them. Both genders must recognize this —

there is no gender better than the other.

In truth, God made them both in tandem to be the roots for a family to rise from. Everything is connected – you only need the eyes to see.

***

When a man came to this earth, he came as a viceroy under god – but he has forgotten this place. We have become divided into race and class, unable to recognize or understand the intrinsic sovereignty of man. We must reclaim the power lost to us – we must reclaim the strength to make our own decisions, follow our own choices, create our own path.

But no King can rule alone; no power exists in a vacuum. Unlike the Machiavellian Prince, the King must be a part of a two-fold alliance – and that is family. Today's system and structures have been tailored by Princes obsessed with power – but the King must rise above, not alone, but with someone else in tow. Someone who has the nobility, strength, and intellect to be his other half.

Someone who stands beside him through the turning of epochs and wonders and horrors of the ages.

Someone who is a reflection so absolute, that there ceases to be any difference between the two

and what is left is a paradigm perhaps more powerful than any other. A paradigm more honest than any other.

And this is what the Believers must grasp and learn from. Your Uncle Me'Shorn has definitely understood this – and I understood it when I married a woman I was destined to spend the rest of my life with. Alone, I was simply a seeker, but with her at my side? We rise as–

King and Queen

> *"When a woman treats a man like a king, and a man treats a woman like a queen, they make one hell of a team"*

Bryan Burden

The Queen is perhaps the most pivotal piece in a game of chess. While the King is, ultimately, the King, he is also extremely vulnerable and limited. Luckily, however, he stands next to the Queen on the board, and the Queen's duty is to protect the King. The Queen-piece can move in any direction, as far as necessary – in a way, the Queen is the binary opposite of the King, but in a way that is effectively complementary rather than competitive.

Now, you might be wondering – why is Uncle Me'Shorn talking about chess? Why is it important?

Well, I'll tell you why it's important – chess is inextricably connected to the human, and indeed, the African Descendant experience. Chess is a game of constructs, white and black, opposing binaries that nonetheless still represent the complexity of alliances and multiplicity; chess is a game that demonstrates and reflects the matrix and the world's paradigms. It represents the constructs we are caught in when we enter this world. We are caught in rules and limitations, like pieces on a chessboard – and this is the trauma of human life.

The Chessboard is an analogy for reality, and to understand the board is vital – to play the game is vital. If we stand in place, hoping for something to occur on its own, it never will, and we'll be left wondering why nothing is happening for us. All those who affect and mask reality with moves of power are players in the game – they are people who understand the board. Today, majority of the players belong to the European demographic, the rich and the wealthy and the powerful, the folk who run the ins and outs of this world as familiarly as jotting down their own names.

Yet this was not always so. Do you know where chess comes from? Let Uncle Me'Shorn tell you – Chess is a game that, in itself, originates from Africa! That's right, it comes from the very place from which came the slaves, the long suffering men and women whose descendant I and so many others are.

Somewhere out in an Egyptian tomb, there is a painting on the tomb of the lady-Pharaoh Nefertiti playing Senat. Now, Senat is a board game that involves the very strategic basis of chess and the struggle of the human condition. But even if you discount the Egyptian folk, look at the other 'leisure games' from that continent. Some games like Wari that are almost seven thousand years old, and in these games, beans or seeds would be used instead of chess pieces. Another game, sometimes called Morels, was played in ancient Egypt. The objective of the game was for players to defeat enemy pieces and block the opponent's moves. Sounds like chess to me.

So prior to becoming slaves, folk knew about all these games – they still had their Queen. Like the Pharaoh's wife playing Senat, our men were Kings while the women played the role of Queen. But when they were taken captive, they were estranged from this tradition; the newly made slaves had lost not just their freedom, lives, and property, but they had also lost their Queen.

It has always been the Colonizer's tool to divide and conquer; the colonizer has always used this tool to divide a people, segregate them, fragmentize their identities, and tear them into squabbling, ineffectual individuals. To alienate the slaves from their Queen was an important part of this scheme – without one's Queen, one can never consider themselves as King. And thus, many descendants of slaves fell into becoming their black. They fell into becoming the colonizer's 'black man', losing sight of the Kings they could have been.

***

But what about the colonizer?

What about the dominant power, the hegemonies? How did they create and maintain their power structure? In truth, they utilized the very tool they alienated the slaves from: the Queen.

What they used is the White Queen. The White Queen is a construct – a woman of European descent enveloped in the color construct. Look throughout history and you will find that the White Queen has been the source of conflict, war, and awe-inspiring scales of ruin. The White Queen is like Helen of Troy; her very presence inspires destruction. Whether she realizes it or not, she has been set up to act as a weapon of ideological warfare.

Now, Uncle Me'Shorn, you say, what's all this talk of white queens? I thought we were denying white and black as being constructs?

Let me explain: I don't use this terminology lightly or with any intent to debase or praise women of European descent. What the phrase 'White Queen' reflects is an analysis of a construct that already exists. There is no other way of referring to it, because women of European descent have been put on this specific pedestal through no fault of their own. I want to make a point here: just because socially, the White Queen construct has consigned European women into this constructed caricature, does not mean they are completely helpless and powerless to resist against it or find a new path.

When I was working as a Surgical Tech, I was a man working in the very heart of an antiseptic, European atmosphere. In fact, when I first stepped into a surgical theatre, the harsh glare of the lights, the burst of antiseptic, the sheer whiteness of the view before me shocked me; the sudden onslaught of images was enough to effectively knock me out. It was only later that I understood it was because my brain had been so overstimulated by this unfamiliar atmosphere.

Working as a Surgical Tech, I was surrounded, as one would be, by nurses – and most of these nurses were 'white women'. They were, in essence, White Queens like I just described – but as I said previously, we always have a choice. We can choose to be what they want us to be – or we can move past it. And just as I reject to be America's black, women caught in the White Queen construct can find a new place for themselves, transcending the demeaning and destructive roles assigned to them by the social order.

One of the examples I can give of such a lady of European descent is a former co-worker, Sue Anne Carrillo. Now Sue Anne and I go way back – she was a civilian nurse whose husband was in the army when we initially met, and was now working as an OR circulator RN. We had worked together multiple times and could attest to each other's competence in the OR. Now, we were periodically given the same patient care assignments for the day. So, we developed a working relationship of trust and respect. In fact, we grew so close as a team, that at work, we were called "work husband and wife!"

Now, after around five years of working together, we were talking and I said something about choosing her to work with as my circulator. That day she explained to me how we really started working together. She told me that, actually, she chose me. As I heard on in surprise, she proceeded to explain how a nurse a long time ago had asked her to trade assignments. Whatever bias this nurse had against me, Sue Anne chose, from her own volition, to go out on a limb and demonstrate that working with me really wasn't bad. She chose to protect me from whatever criticism the other nurse had for me, and indirectly, had been doing so for years – shielding me from women who seemed to find any honest expression of masculinity to be 'toxic'. At work, Sue Anne stepped in as my queen.

Now, Sue Anne wasn't 'the American black'.

She did not look like me, and she did not belong to the same chain of ancestors as me. Yet, nonetheless, she chose to stand for me, and act as my Queen. Understand that even though she was, at the end of day, not my actual Queen, she still chose to act in my benefit. Indirectly, she joined the struggle – indirectly, she acted against the paradigms binding us. On the chessboard of 'white' against 'black', she acted in a way that was completely unforeseen and unexpected from a 'White Queen'; she acted against the role prescribed for her in the rules!

And this is the latent power of these 'White Queens' that America has objectified, used, and turned into token diversification quotas. The liberal-democratic world continues to 'make spaces' for these women, just as they continue to 'make spaces' for their black – but these spaces are prison cells, and no prison lasts forever.

The women of European descent that have been imprisoned in their ivory tower, on their pedestal of silver and chalk, cannot remain there indefinitely. The dam will shatter; the flood shall be let loose. There is a path ahead, a destiny that the White Queen may yet follow, and it is a path utterly unimaginable for those who have 'created' her as a tool.

Only a fool underestimates how much power they hold – and how unimaginable the consequences can be for the ruling elite.

Remember, America – I am not yours.

And remember, America – the White Queen is not yours.

***

But ultimately, the American Descendants of Slaves have mostly, throughout the years, remained alienated from their other half. Our communities have been populated by men who are more like wandering gypsies than Kings, sad, fickle, and flighty people who cannot put down their roots – because they have no roots. They have been stripped away from them, and now, menfolk wander from woman to woman, unable to settle down or own up to their children. As I related before, the trauma of having a father who refuses to accept you, a father who would have had you aborted, is something deeply scarring. And these scars have continued through the years, creating broken households and torn families.

The family, as I said before, depends on Man and Woman – not just in a specific instance, but in all instances. It is the oldest bond, the very first bond. There is no human relationship as old as Man and Woman. When Adam and Eve fell unto the earth, they came as viceroys, as King and Queen of the wretched earth under the watchful eye of Heaven.

What did they come to earth with? Nothing, except each other. And this is what we, as a community, have lost – the other half. Man and woman have become segregated, living apart in the same neighborhoods. Even in the same household, on average, there is a split between the Man and Woman. Under the American roof, the sacred bond is turned into a piece of whimsy to be discarded at will, toyed with as needed.

In that respect, your Uncle Me'Shorn has been more fortunate than most. After I spoke in tongues that night on the road and was reborn, I was fortunate enough to find a woman who was nothing short of made for me. Without a doubt, I knew that she was my Queen.

I had discovered prior, in my first marriage, that I could not have children – though we did have an adopted foster-daughter. Ultimately, however, me and my first wife drifted apart on account of the epiphany I had undergone. No longer could I join her in the darkness – Like the wise men of old, I had seen the truth and could not return.

The way I first heard of my wife was through a mutual friend – but I first talked to her through coincidence. I had not called her before, despite our mutual friend having given me her number, but the moment I heard her voice, I knew we had to meet. And meet we did, having never seen each other before – and I was awestruck. The moment I saw her, I knew it in my heart that this woman was my Queen.

We married on the 4th of October, 1996.

Unlike my first marriage, when I had felt constantly alienated and discomforted, on the day of this wedding, I felt genuinely, spiritually liberated. Looking into my wife's eyes, I knew I had discovered what it truly meant to be more than just a man – though I did not know what to call it then, it was the sensation of first realizing that I was a King. I was not a pawn, pushed forward to my doom, nor a knight to loyally obey orders, nor a bishop to be thrown far and wide.

I was the King, vulnerable but vital. I was not a bystander, or a servant.

I, Me'Shorn T. Daniels, was in the game.

***

The thing about the King and Queen is that they are not just two separate identities – they actually and actively complete each other.

They individual unit is actually a half, which is

why the individualistic ideology furthered by liberalism is inherently and totally flawed. The individual can never achieve true enlightenment or self-sustainability because he or she is designed to exist in pairs. It is this truth that has been easily and steadfastly ignored by modern America, leaving behind a host of ruined people with identity disorders. An example of the true nature of the King and Queen is to be found in Asian philosophy and religion: the concept of Yin and Yang.

Yin is negative, dark, and feminine, while Yang is positive, bright, and masculine. As can be seen. these concepts are in binary opposition – yet their interaction influences the destinies of all things and creatures. Yin and Yang are utterly different, yet they work in concert – they are directly opposed to each other, yet they work together.

There is no Yin without Yang, nor Yang without Yin; one is needed for the other to be meaningful.

Thus, just as a Queen needs to have a King to have any claim to sovereignty, the King needs to have a Queen to keep being a King. There is no singular sovereignty – there must be no egoism between the two. If one leaves, the bond collapses

and like a fission reaction, the splitting of the bond is like the splitting of the atom, with disastrous consequences.

***

The following is a portion written by Queen Azizza Maryam Muhammad regarding me. Now, it represents her perspectives on who I am, but again, it is her perspective.

Yet, I have always believed in letting others have their viewpoint, and express themselves fully and honestly – and in the interest of that spirit, here is Queen Azizza.

"THE MAKING"

"When I think of Me'Shorn Floyd Daniels, I think of a mountain that I was able to witness being built. I encountered him on social media and had seen many post from him but never actually interacted with him. Then came the invitation to Descendants of American Slaves and I said to myself…WOW. Finally there were other people in the world that wanted to recognize and honor them as much as I did but I never could come up with a name that I felt was appropriate to do so and I certainly NEVER wanted to use the word "slaves". How sophisticated was that name and what an honor to the ancestors.

Upon hearing his voice for the first time as he introduced me to what I call the Military Crew which consisted of Marcus, Leonard and Jacie. He introduced them with their military titles and was so proud to do so as if to impress me. At the time he had no idea of how I viewed the military and nor did I give off the vibe that I was not impressed but I really wasn't. I was more interested in what was about to become of the organization DASI and how I could play a part in what I believed was going to be something big, something great. His voice was loud and he almost roared when he spoke and his level of excitement was astounding. I really didn't understand the hype but I rolled with it because it was at that point that I realized that there were many many layers to that voice on the other end of the phone. Finally we got to the business at hand and before long I was apart of this distinguished group of men , of brothers and I adored them and I was proud of them and I respected them. Needless to say, things didn't go as I hoped but at the same time there was that bond I formed with Me'Shorn and in my heart he was and is my brother. I had the honor to speak to his bonus father Mr. Charles Daniels and I began to understand all of the layers that made a man like Me'Shorn. We share the same family name, our American family history began in the same place and I wondered could we be related. Then he dropped a bombshell on me and explained that Charles Daniels was actually his step father and that his biological father was nowhere around, EVER. It was at that moment I realized the beginning of the making of Me'Shorn Floyd- Daniels and the journey that his development took.

    There were many conversations, disagreements, conflict and changes and I expected more from him and better of him. I had come to realize that this man was all over the place and that the creative aspect of him had taken over his life. He worked a full time job, has a full time marriage, he had adult aged children and he lead many many organizations and before I knew it I was appointed and admitted into so many groups and so many organizations that I simply could not keep up nor did I want to. As I slowly witnessed the deterioration of Descendants of American Slaves Inc. my heart was breaking because I knew that within the name itself there lied a solution to "Black" life and that going from Black life to African American life was more than a name change but it was a movement. I already had a whole network named Nation Building Movement and I somehow had to find a way to link the two together but my Military Crew had done a complete about face on my hopes and I was ANGRY and unforgiving at that point at all of them but especially Me'Shorn because he was the one that took me to the apex of my hopes and let me fall with no security to hoist me up . It was over two years before I would speak a single word to him Leonard, Marcus and Jacie and to this day I have yet to speak to Marcus and Jacie about what was or what could have been. The dream remained as time passed and we all were on different journeys.

  One day the phone rang and it was Me'Shorn Daniels and I said to myself it was time for a confrontation but I had no energy for that and time moved about as if there was never a hiccup in the relationship or bond that we had formed.

  Although conflict may still exist around DASI there is something bigger and greater and that is simply love for the brotherhood. There is a saying in the Holy Quran that says "We pass from death to life when we have love for the brotherhood" and I live my life in that manner. Always forgiving and always seeking understanding instead of revenge or even reckoning. I rather take the atonement approach which is good for all of us.

More recently there was an examination of Me'Shorn. He is older now and still that high spirit remains. That roar in his voice remains, that determination remains, and I realized that there was no real peace within and that peace had long abandoned this brother and I finally was able to see why.

There has always been this homage paid to the

U.S. Military which I was never a fan but surely I respected what they did but not always what the men and women became in the process and I see the effects that it has had on many people and I can now clearly see the effects that it HAS on Me'Shorn Daniels. This man has credited the US Army with fostering him into manhood and that a beating by the historical Black Panthers was a significant milestone into this journey of going from a boy to a man. I hear constantly about how becoming an E-7 in the Army has been his greatest accomplishment in LIFE only because this is an honor given by the president of the united states. Why didn't I use the proper punctuation in the previous sentence? Well let's explore why   The president at the time was Bill Clinton who has admitted that he helped design the methodology of incarcerating African American men and women to heavy and extremely lengthy prison sentences for possession and the manufacturing of crack cocaine while the caucasian population that possessed a more potent powdered form of cocaine receive a slap on the wrist. Why did I not capitalize the words united states, simple   we

are NOT united nor have we ever been. Still there is Me'Shorn who clearly recognizes the history of African slaves. The slaves from Africa were never apart of the America that the caucasians intended. They were brought to this soil to serve like a horse for transportation or a mule for heavy hauling or like the human cotton gin. Never to be an equal participant or owner or have opportunities to freedom, justice, and equality. Still for Me'Shorn he has a love for the institution of the military because he honestly believes that in some way it was his savior and he shouts it loud and proud.

In conversations there is the redundant tales of his experiences in the military. He takes every opportunity to credit the Army for lessons learned, for development, even for the creation of his own manhood and if you don't have an ear to listen you will never comprehend his existence. The roar and loudness of his voice says something, the stories of being promoted to an E-7 in the Army says something, the constant mentioning of manhood is saying something but very few that know him hear it. Pain and past trauma is often masked by behavior. Me'Shorn's behavior tells a story . There is a NEED to be seen by the world as the epitome of MANHOOD because trauma has called him to question himself as to how he's viewed in the eyes of others, wondering if others could see the trauma and if they knew what the trauma was would he still be viewed as a man.

Abuse plagues so many people all over the world. Abuse opens the eyes of people to witness how far away we are from our moral authority and how far we are from God and when we suffer abuse at the hands of one who should love and care for us it is so much harder to escape the horror of it all. Combine that with abandonment by one who is suppose to love and guide you and you have then created a broken person, one who is divided internally with one side desiring justice and reckoning and the other side desiring love and peace. The creative victims can hide this well to never allow you to figure it out so to speak but the signs are there. With Me'Shorn he replaced his lack of having a male parent with the Army, he replaces abandonment with creations of organizations that SHOULD get attention, and note that most of them surround the pursuit of manhood or at the least the mentioning of it.

Is Me'Shorn a complicated individual? No, he is a man that has replaced pain with passion and the methods he uses to be seen can be extreme at times. The constant accreditation of the U.S. Military with being his father, the constant loud talking to be overbearing because men should be heard and his testicles should come through his voice. The need to agitate causes and be seen but to be seen as a REAL man is the most important thing in his entire world.

What is the truth of Me'Shorn is that he has yet to realize who he really is. He is like every Black Man in America because until you recognize and realize your African Americanism you will always force yourself against what is so very natural and so easy to obtain within. What I wish for him is that he gives himself some credit for having the courage to simply stand and stare pain, trauma, and challenges in the face and conquer the obstacles that attempted to stand in his way and know that before he belonged to his mother, his father, his bonus father, his children, his wife, this world, he first belonged to the God that created him and had pre-ordered his steps in this world. It is not about being loud and proud but it is about making things happen just as God has shown us.

Say "be" and it becomes and it is. Me'Shorn is my brother in spirit and in truth and it is that truth that I see in him that proves that he has never really been a regular Black man but he is African in every way but when you credit those that try to destroy you and when you allow trauma to make you feel inadequate or less than, it shows that you have forgotten the creator and his power to bring you peace in the depths of your heart and that is what I desire the most for him." (written by Queen Azizza Maryam Muhammad)

***

And this is what I champion; King and Queen, together. Even if our narratives vary, even if her story of Who I Am varies from my own, even if her assessment of me is wildly different from mine – she is still my Queen, and I am still her King. This is the bond that has been lost; this is the understanding that is under threat here.

We have seen the apocalyptic hell that the ancestors have endured when they were colonized, stripped of all culture and identities, and forced into slavery. The segregation of the Queen from the King has led to his downfall – and though there is no way to go back, there must be a push to continue.

To all folk part of the ADS (American Descendants of Slaves), I say this: we cannot fight alone. We cannot be a disparate group of would-be revolutionaries. We cannot continue to keep being lonely, individual warriors. Not even the three wise men came to Christ alone – we must bind together, and most importantly, we must bind ourselves, our very souls, to another. Someone who can support you, someone willing to carry the burden.

Listen when I say that we must regain our Kingship.

We must find our Queens.

We must become our true selves. We must keep–

Moving Forward

"What's done is done. What's gone is gone. One of life's lessons is always moving on. It's okay to look back to see how far you've come, but keep moving forward."

Roy T. Bennett

I expect that when the Wise men set off in the search for the Messiah, there would have been moments of self-doubt, of hardship, of obstacles in their path. I imagine they would have stood in the sweltering sun and felt that moment of utter desolation – and yet, that moment never deterred them. In fact, it made their resolve stronger, and despite that little voice telling them to give up and go home, they knew there was no return. All they could do was to keep moving forward.

When one sees the shambles of America, it is natural to desire a solution. It is natural to desire a conclusion to this chaos, an end to the violence and sensual depravities, but this end cannot be achieved through myths. It cannot be achieved through a promise of return. It cannot be achieved through gratuitous backtracking.

The families that have suffered from neglect, distance, abuse, abandonment, poverty, sicknesses, and a host of depravities cannot simply be remade in an ideal image. Time cannot turn back, and the hourglass of the universe does not run the other way around. Instead, we must all continue to live in the shadow of a past that looms ever-larger, eternally looking down upon us. But we must not look back – our eyes must be fixed forward, upon the elusive horizon of the future.

I will never regain the innocence I lost in my youth. Children who have been abused will never be able to undo that damage. Mankind will never return to the state it fell from. And yet – we can ensure that the future is saved by our sacrifice. It falls upon people like me and you to protect the innocence of children, to ensure that the horrors in our pasts are never repeated. We must ensure that our trauma does not afflict our families, that we do not pass the curse over to our children and youth. Patterns of generational trauma must be broken, or we run the risk of losing another generation from the same abyss that we have barely managed to crawl out of.

Sure, the damage is done for now to our societies, but we can rebuild. We can sow the seeds for a better future – and Man reaps what he sows. If today, we sow the seeds of an ideal family, create an enduring belief and faith in values that would be beneficial to America in the long run, eventually the yield of our efforts would bloom in earnest. Eventually, we would be able to create a precedent whereupon the successive generations will base their beliefs, upon which the reformers of tomorrow will act. There is a Chinese proverb: The journey of many miles begins with a single step.

We must take that step.

Instead of trying to regress to a mythical, pastoral America with fields of wheat and jobs galore, we should be trying to achieve those things in actuality! The myth never existed, but the future is a blank canvas, and we may make of it what we choose. America was never great, but we can choose to Make America Greater Than It Ever Was. This idea, what I also call MAGTIEW, runs antithetical to all promises and appeals to return. All I believe in is making the best possible future for myself, my family, my people, and my country.

You've never treated me all that well, America

but even though I refuse to be yours, a part of me still loves you. I am still a patriot, and I may be your wayward son, but I am among the very few who actually care for you. I am among those august few who want to move forward with you instead of being lost in some false nostalgia – I am among the few who believe in placing the first bricks that will become the shining towers of tomorrow.

So to all my fellow Americans, Uncle Me'Shorn has this to say: Help me make America the great country we know she can be.

Help make American greater than it's ever been.
***

When we move forward, we abandon many things behind us. These may be things we are used to, things we are attached to, or things we think we need.

But the point of continuing to move forward is to continue to improve. Imagine if you continued to act in a rebellious, adolescent manner as a fully grown adult – you would be seen as strange and maladjusted! Human beings live through time linearly – we have been designed to continue to keep moving forward, continuing to develop, evolve, and change. We all go through phases in our lives, phases in our mental, spiritual, material, or academic experiences – and all of these phases and changes are what continue to make us better, improved versions of ourselves. If we can look back on our lives and see the flaws of our past selves, it means that we have improved since then.

Change is an important part of one's life, and it is an important part of the growth and health of any society. The paradigms infecting America have been designed in a way that prioritizes 'progress' but, in fact, never allows any progress at all. All the liberal agenda actually accomplishes is a regression to a primal, visceral state of existence – from civilized people, we are incentivized to return to the violent delights and sexual debauchery of a savage, uncultured life.

This is why America has no culture – despite

being called 'bigoted' and a 'cause of disparity', culture and tradition are naturally prone to change. All cultures and traditions have slowly shifted and changed over time – but in America, culture does not exist in any pure state. In fact, it has been stamped out, replaced by a colorful semblance of it that makes for a bad copy. It is a corporate, soulless copy of tradition – the 'ethnocultural richness' I observed in Louisville was about as far as one can get from culture. While real culture and tradition provide societies with a sense of direction, a way to move ahead, the liberal construct that has replaced it is purely aesthetic, acting as a funnel to lead mankind back to its darkest and most primal desires.

It is a regression in the name of progress, a fall in the name of diversity. If all mankind does is play around in a colorful, plastic pleasure garden, there is no moving ahead – there is no W.O.R.K – and there is no reward. We must reject the temptation of the ideal pleasures offered by the modern world, and realize how fleeting these pleasures are – we must realize that like the wanderers and dervishes of old, we must not be tempted away from our purpose, which is to move ever-closer to the truth, like moths drawn to the eternal flame. As men consigned to life, it falls upon us as a solemn duty to W.O.R.K. and earn our keep on this earth.

Uncle Me'Shorn does not believe in surrender.

I do not believe in despair. I do not believe in being helpless in the face of the age we live in. I believe in change; bringing it, experiencing it, and applying it to the world around us.

Most of all, I believe in mankind, because I still believe in the humanist ideals this country once promised to follow. I believe in the human ability to build something from nothing. Our ability to

compartmentalize our troubles and traumas, and to keep on, keeping on. And when the going gets tough, remember Uncle Me'Shorn's words:

Keep looking ahead. Keep moving forward.

***

When I decry temptation, don't think that I don't understand it – hell, there was a time when even your Uncle Me'Shorn was caught up in a web of earthly pleasures and promiscuity.

But as I grew and evolved as a man and as a person, I came to the realization that these fleeting pleasures meant nothing. There was neither life, nor vitality, nor purpose to these exchanges in the night; as long as a man continues to give into his baser instincts for a momentary release, he continues to be caught in a loop, and it is a loop many can never escape from. You end up addicted to the thrill, but there is no meaning or purpose to it. There is no one there to move ahead with, nor someone who can pull you up when you're down, or push you ahead when you falter; there are only wraiths in the night that are holding you in place, even as you try to escape.

What a King needs is not pleasure. What a king needs is not momentary satisfaction, nor the promise thereof; a King needs a Queen. And this is why a Queen is so vital – a Queen is someone who will move forward with you. She will empower, strengthen, and vitalize your soul when you are down, protect you when you're oblivious, and accompany you as you grow, evolve, and go through the phases of personhood.

My first Wife could not stay as my Queen because she could not move forward with me. She looked at life a certain way, and I looked at it in another way entirely – and our perspectives did not match at all. We were two different people, with different goals and aims. Such a relationship can never be the basis of something truly meaningful – I think the bear minimum between man and wife should be agreement to move forward, together. When we vow in a marriage to never part, we make that vow because it is difficult. Marriage is meant to be a trial, but sitting around together in the same intellectual phase forever is easy. Easy, but unrewarding – there is, again, no purpose to it.

A King and his Queen adopt the nobler path.

They walk through the desert together, their souls intertwined around the same purpose, around the same desire to continue to move ahead toward a shared aim. They continue to help each other grow and expand their understanding of the world they inhabit; they help each other attain their fullest, truest potential instead of being a hindrance. What we all need isn't someone to hold us back or anchor us down – we need someone who continues to motivate, inspire, and accompany you through life's journey.

Again, I have been very fortunate in this regard. My wife, my Queen, has supported me through all of these endeavors. The epiphanies I have undergone, the realizations I have had, would have been completely repressed and killed off if they happened to another man, with a partner uninterested in the truth. Yet, in this marriage, I have been blessed with someone who walks alongside me, and someone who continues to move forward instead of being lost in the present or past.

What differentiates a King and Queen from others is that they are players. They are playing upon the very chessboard that traps others, and this element of play requires you to think in chess – which is to say, I think in terms of the future. If one plays chess with the present or past moves in mind, one will inevitably lose, because the objective of the game is to anticipate what will come next. This means that the entire point of the game is to look forward and not backward; the point is to realize the linearity of the game, the fact that moves can only be made, but never unmade. The game must be played no matter what, no matter how much we regret the move in question.

Chess teaches us to accept the moves we made, and keep playing. That is a truth that holds similarly true in life; and this is why we must become the

Kings and Queens we were meant to be. We must be tacticians and strategists, carefully commanding the future from the present, accepting and learning from the past, even as our roots give us the strength and stability to continue our great endeavor.

From the past, come our roots.

In the present, we make our moves. For tomorrow, we W.O.R.K.

***

Ultimately, to continue to move forward is my aim, but one day, I hope to see the sun rise on a better America. I hope to see my struggles end in a dawn as beautiful as the one most people merely fantasize about – and I hope to see my aims come to fruition.

But even if the consequences of this struggle come far into the future, your Uncle Me'Shorn remains optimistic. For every struggle, there is a beginning and an ending – and we spend our lives traveling from one to another. And as we keep moving forward, inevitably there is a destination, but as important as the destination is what comes after – which is memory. For all that we accomplish, all that we are on our short time on earth, leaves behind a legacy. No family ever ends, no individual ever truly dies; we all leave behind our W.O.R.K. when we pass from this world, and it lies there in wait for another to take up the burden.

In the end, our legacies transcend all–

Part V
Endings

Epilogue

"There is no real ending. It's just the place where you stop thestory."

Frank Herbert.

And so, we come upon the end – or rather, where I choose to stop this book. I think if you're saying anything that's worth saying, you can always say more about it, write more about it, add more to it, but at some point, the most important thing is where you choose to stop.

But even endings happen in stages – nothing stops immediately, and nothing ends forever. Even after an ending, there comes an epilogue – and After-Ending, a reckoning that comes after the text is done talking. In one sense, this chapter is the epilogue for this book, but in a realer sense, your life is the real epilogue for this text. Everything you have read in this book is only the first hint of the depth of Uncle Me'Shorn's beliefs – it is only a seed, but it may yet grow into an epiphany. I certainly hope it does, for this land of false idols could really use an epiphany.

For your sake, America, I hope you take my words to heart. When I started writing this book, I started with six simple words: I Am Not Your Black,

America. This was the essence of what I had to say, and I have said it with all my heart, with all the honest indignation in my soul: I reject your labels.

Now the ball falls in your court. How does my rejection make you feel? How do you react to it? For you, I have always been a 'black man' – now that you know that I am not, who do you see me as? Let me tell you how I hope to be seen – I hope that you see me as Uncle Me'Shorn – a man who has lived his years on this earth, seen many things, learnt many things, and had realizations that would make other men wilt. I have looked into the abyss of this country's heart and I have emerged from that darkness with a new light in my eyes, a new aim in my mind. I have emerged like the wanderers of old, desiring nothing but to travel towards the truth, slowly and inexorably drawn to the actuality of things like a moth to flame.

The paradigms that envelop this country are imagined by people who disregard the consequences – what matters to them is to create blanket ideologies that guide the overall shape of society into what they deem to be right. These people in their ivory towers look down upon the social order with the benefit of distance; from that high up, all they see is their plans succeeding, constructs woven into each other like an ideological tapestry. Yet what these people do not see, what they do not realize from their alienated position of privilege, is that you cannot see dirt and grime from a thousand miles away; while they see success, the common man like yours truly is the one who grows acquainted with the cost of this success – it is the common man who faces the consequence.

Your Uncle Me'Shorn is a man who grew up in the cradle of naught but consequences. I am a man who, from the moment I opened my eyes, have seen the horrific consequences of the color construct, the false Great America, and a matrix of paradigms that has normalized the immoral and accepted the depraved. Hell hath no horror compared to the horror of a society gone wrong – this is a truth that I subconsciously realized at a young age, though I did not yet have the words to express it.

In this current climate of debauchery, falsehoods, and excess, American society is running, is hurtling towards a terrible end – but this ending does not have to be fire and brimstone. All America needs is to bring these runaway paradigms to an end; this country must unlearn its falsehoods so it can relearn the truth. The false America that has tarnished the very values it stands for must end for a new, greater America to rise like a phoenix; America must become Greater Than It Ever Was.

***

Listen to Uncle Me'Shorn, America: make use of your T.O.O.L.S. Your limitations, your bindings, and your challenges are obvious; there is only one way to oppose, and indeed, transcend them. America must regain its spiritual heart; it must regain its soul. Limitations are intrinsically material; paradigms are intrinsically a product of the world. They are a product of human minds, flesh and blood, products of thinking and artifice. The spiritual is the doorway to reality – it is the only way to escape the artificial, material limitations that bind the American citizen.

In a society where our communities are bound in the nets of a false American faith, an alienating color construct, and a policy of segregation of man from woman and King from Queen, rearming ourselves with our T.O.O.L.S is vital. American Descendants of Slaves, African Americans aware of their roots, must find the faith within themselves. There is no preacher, no sermon out there that can magically give you this faith – it must come from within, from the fount of epiphany. Uncle Me'Shorn promises you this – epiphany is not a hard thing to find for the honest Seeker, for the Seeker is meant for the search. A man who leaves his house like a wanderer of old seeking Christ is bound to come into epiphany.

Nothing, not even spiritual awakening, comes without effort. Unlike the sparrow provided for by the Lord, we have fallen from that state of carefree innocence – all our aims and objectives upon this earth can only be achieved through W.O.R.K. As I realized that fateful day upon the road, the Lord wasn't done with me yet. There was more that I needed to do, and there was more that I needed to say; and although my work in general will never end as long as I exist on this here earth, to continue to try is necessary.

It is a fallacy to think that epiphany is the end of your journey – in fact, it is the beginning.

Likewise, this book, and this epilogue, will not end when you put it down. This book is only the start – it is like the seeds sown into the earth, and we all sow what we reap.

For America, I hope that this book acts as a catalyst, as a first step to ushering this country into a better future, and leave behind the mistakes of the past.

***

Above all else, America, realize this: there are no white lives. There are no black lives. There are only the lives given unto man by God, and all of them matter.

God's Lives Matter is a movement that believes essentially in this – and it is a movement that I hope more listen to. There has been too much death, too much chaos to continue to remain mired in paradigms while we sale towards an uncertain end. As long as we continue to 'other' and disregard each other, as long as we continue to build narratives of constant, harmful self- affirmation, we will be stuck in this cycle of hate.

We must come together, all of us – and for such a day to dawn, I wait.

I am not your black, America. You do not dictate the life given unto me by God; you do not dictate the essential value of my existence. No man or woman can. My life is neither more, nor less valuable than any other man, woman, or child in this country, in this whole world. All lives have infinite value. Ultimately, all I am working towards, all I believe in, is a world free of labels, a world free of false identities, and a world free of the horrors you've wrought in the name of class, color, and creed. For those who still ask who I am to say what is right: Am I not a man and brother, America? Do I not have a say? This is a democratic nation built upon the very ideals of humanism; I have every right to speak my peace, America.

And if a word from Uncle Me'Shorn can inspire a single soul, or give purpose to a single brother or sister, then yes, it is a word worth saying.

***

I still pray for you, America.

I pray that one day, you find your path. That one day, you find a way past the limitations you have set for yourself. I hope that one day, men and women of all classes and creeds share a table under the heavens, united in spirit; I hope that you find yourself a destiny worth fulfilling. There is much that is wrong with you, but there is much that I still want to love – may you become the nation I wish to love.

I am not your black, America – but you are still my country, the country I served and continue to serve. May you hear my cries, and may the fruit of my W.O.R.K. bring some peace unto you.

Amen and hallelujah, Your Uncle Me'Shorn.

Appendix

Inverted Order of Fruits of Spirit

Galatians 5:22-23

New International Version

22 But the fruit of the Spirit is love, joy, peace, forbearance, kindness, goodness, faithfulness, 23 gentleness and self-control. Against such things there is no law.
I had a revelation that I should invert the order in which fruits of spirit was written in the Bible.
Self-control, gentleness, faithfulness, goodness, Kindness, forbearance, peace, and love.
Also, that the color orange represents all of the fruits of Spirit.

Uncle MeShorn

www.UncleMeShorn.com

www.ingramcontent.com/pod-product-compliance
Lightning Source LLC
LaVergne TN
LVHW031611060526
838201LV00065B/4804